IT'S NOT RIGHT-LEFT,
IT'S TOP-DOWN

Enjoy the book!

All the best,

IT'S NOT RIGHT-LEFT, IT'S TOP-DOWN

THE TRUTH ABOUT THE MEDIA

OWEN MAGEAU

NEW DEGREE PRESS

COPYRIGHT © 2021 OWEN MAGEAU

All rights reserved.

IT'S NOT RIGHT-LEFT, IT'S TOP-DOWN
The Truth about the Media

ISBN   978-1-63676-834-2   *Paperback*

           978-1-63730-208-8   *Kindle Ebook*

           978-1-63730-278-1   *Ebook*

This book is dedicated to my loving grandma, Harolyn Mageau, who sadly passed away in July of 2020. She was the person I could always count on to listen to me and be supportive. No matter what I did, my grandma always told me she was impressed. If it wasn't for her constant support, there is no way I would have ever had the confidence to imagine I could write a book. Thank you, Grandma. I love you, and I hope I've impressed you once again.

CONTENTS

"*Journalists are made aware of where the channel or the network organization's priorities are. It is made clear to them, don't fuck with the piggy bank, or the people who are buttering your bread.*"

DAVID SHUSTER, FORMER JOURNALIST AT
MSNBC, CNN, AND THE FOX NEWS CHANNEL

INTRODUCTION

―――

"Walmart is a major advertiser here on MSNBC. I'm not telling you not to do the story because I would never tell any of my journalists whether to do a story or not to do a story. I'm simply asking if you would consider not doing it because of a lot of sensitivities on the business side of the company."

This is what David Shuster said the president of MSNBC, Phil Griffin, said to him when Shuster pitched a segment for his show that reflected on Walmart in a negative light.

After thinking long and hard about it, Shuster decided they wouldn't run the story about Walmart. His reasoning was it wasn't a massive breaking news story and for his own sake, he didn't think it was worth it to go against his boss.

"I think if it had been a major story or something where we were moving the ball, I would have said, 'No, we're doing the story,' but it wasn't a lead story, so it just felt like, okay, I will give one to the boss here, so maybe I will get a chip down the road," Shuster said.

If you've ever wondered if you're getting an objective, wholesome picture of what is going on in the world from the mainstream news outlets in the United States, the answer is you simply aren't. As showcased in this short, simple story David Shuster shared with me from his time as an anchor at MSNBC, the structure of the news media in this country is set up to cater to the interests of its corporate owners and advertisers, not to report the objective truth.

Since Donald Trump entered the race for the 2016 Republican Nomination for President of the United States, the term "Fake News" has become very popular. The former president is famous for calling media organizations that are critical of him fake news and insulting them in other ways.

"Your organization is terrible; I am not going to give you a question. You are fake news." That's what then-President-elect Donald Trump said to CNN correspondent Jeff Acosta during a press conference after being elected president in 2016.[1] Trump refused to take Acosta's question, and this wasn't the last time he would do something like this. Trump, along with a sizeable sector of the population, cry fake news whenever they see something they don't like or agree with.

Many people have rightfully fought back against these claims of fake news; however, these same people have fell victim to the same behavior. People who opposed Trump now tend to call anything that praises or praised the former president fake news as well.

---

1   Kelsey Sutton, "Trump Calls CNN 'Fake News,' as Channel Defends Its Reporting on Intelligence Briefing," *Politico*, January 11, 2017.

Our society has become extremely polarized with one group, largely republicans, believing everything Fox News says and calling everything that comes from MSNBC and CNN fake news, while the other side does just the opposite. Democrats tend to believe everything reported by MSNBC or CNN, whereas they lament Fox News.

America has always been divided, but this increase in polarization is extremely problematic because the reality of the situation is these networks are much more similar than they are different. This party loyalty, loyalty to the home team, and loyalty to their preferred network causes people to focus on the deficiencies of the opposing side, all the while turning a blind eye to the many deficiencies in the outlets they themselves find to be reputable news sources. This dynamic leads to both sides having a distorted view of the truth, and that is not a good thing. It leads to a much more hostile environment because people aren't grounded in facts. It's one thing, a good thing, to discuss and argue about different policies or ideas, as long as we all agree on the basic facts. However, this isn't the case anymore. Americans don't even agree on what is fact and what is fiction. It eliminates the possibility of finding common ground, and this is a frightening development.

The bottom line is all of the mainstream networks aren't providing their consumers with the whole story. So everyday Americans must stop fighting with one another and calling each other stupid, uneducated, brainwashed, or whatever else it may be. If you get your news from Fox, your enemy isn't the people who watch MSNBC or CNN. If you watch MSNBC or CNN, your enemy isn't the people who watch Fox. It's time to wake up and see we're all being conned. We should not be each other's enemy, but it should be the system of corporate ownership that incentivizes these networks not to report the full accurate version of every story.

Don't believe me? If you have a family to support, mortgage or rent to pay, don't want to lose your employer-sponsored healthcare (if you're lucky enough to have it), and the many other financial responsibilities Americans face, would you openly contradict your bosses? Would you walk into their office and tell them to screw themselves? Would you tell them they're bad people and tell them all the bad things they do? Probably not, because you'd be sent packing, and you'd be looking for another job with the notion you're not a team player following you around.

Journalists face this exact dilemma every time they go to work. They have to choose between reporting the complete, objective story, or complying with the desires of their corporate bosses.

Shuster has previously worked at all three of the major cable news networks, those being CNN, Fox News, and MSNBC, so he knows how the mainstream media operates in the United States. Shuster said all the journalists who have been in the business for a couple of years are apprised of where their channel or network organization's priorities are.

"It is made clear to them, don't fuck with the piggy bank, or the people who are buttering your bread," Shuster said.

We can't fault the journalists. We can say it's immoral to lie or to bury certain stories, but they're only doing their jobs.

What we can fault is the system: the structure of corporate ownership that prevents our news media from being truly objective.

"Once upon a time in the news business, you were given credit for being a hard-nosed journalist who would ask tough questions of everybody," Shuster said. "Now, when you have so many corporate and money-making agendas, and that mix between advertising and the awareness journalists have of the funding, you move up in the business not by seeking out the truth and being aggressive about it, but by swimming in the direction your bosses want the company to swim. So, it's very hard in this day and age, if you are an independent, hard-charging, report- like-hell journalist, to find you have got a future at mainstream broadcast outlets in particular."

The mainstream news media has a vast amount of power in this country. They can shape the public discourse in any way they please, and they can shape the outcomes of elections. The most recent 2020 Democratic primary election was a perfect example of this. When it looked like Vermont Senator Bernie Sanders was poised to run away with the nomination after a landslide victory in Nevada, the mainstream media brought then former vice president Joe Biden back from the dead by affording him the equivalent of an estimated seventy-two million dollars of free positive media in the lead up to Super Tuesday.[2]

---

2   Joshua Cho, "Corporate Media Drove Joe Biden to Victory – but Claims It Doesn't Really Exist," *Salon*, April 25, 2020.

This obscene amount of positive coverage helped to slingshot Biden into the nomination, and in the process, it stopped Sanders, who was leading a movement that threatened the interests of corporate elites, like higher-ups at Comcast, AT&T, and Fox Corporation, the owners of MSNBC, CNN, and Fox News Channel respectively.[3] [4] [5]

It was outlined in the Constitution of the United States we have a right to a free press, but sadly, that is not the case today.[6] The news in this country is not the watchdog of the Constitution looking out for the interests of everyday Americans, but it can be with a few simple changes to the news media's structure in this country.

That is why I wrote this book. We as Americans deserve a news media that is beholden to us and our interests, not the interests of their wealthy owners. Journalists shouldn't be afraid to "fuck with the piggy bank," to save their own jobs. They should be able to follow the truth and report like hell, no matter where it takes them. It is what would be the best for the average American, and therefore the United States as a whole.

---

3   Zacks, "Your Complete Guide to Everything Owned by Comcast," *Nasdaq, Inc.,* October 12, 2017.

4   Rachel Sandler and Skye Gould, "Here's Everything AT&T Will Own after It Buys TimeWarner," *Business Insider,* June 14, 2018.

5   Meg James, "Must Reads: Murdoch Family Launches a New Fox and Former House Speaker Paul Ryan Joins Its Board," *Los Angeles Times,* March 19, 2019.

6   U.S. Const. amend. I.

We don't have to be doomed to a future that consists of our news media lying to us. We can get a media that fights for the truth and is beholden to us. In this book, I outline how we can do this.

PART 1

A FREE PRESS

CHAPTER 1

A FREE PRESS

The right to a free press has always been viewed as a fundamental component of American freedom, but do we actually have a free press?

It was December 15, 1791, when the right to a free press was adopted as part of the first amendment in the United States Bill of Rights.[7] The Founding Fathers of the United States thought the right to a free press was essential for liberty.[8] The foundation for their ideas of liberty and the right to a free press came from the British government's attempt to censor negative information and opinions from being published in newspapers in the original colonies.[9]

---

7   "The Bill of Rights: How Did It Happen?," *The US National Archives and Record Administration*, December 14, 2018.

8   Christina Barron, "No Monument for Madison. But One of His Legacies Is Freedom of the Press," *The Washington Post*, March 14, 2017.

9   Joseph M. Adelman, "Mobilizing the Public against Censorship, 1765 and 2012," *The Atlantic*, January 23, 2012.

To prevent the new American government from becoming too much like the British government, the government they believed to be tyrannical, too powerful, and who they had just fought a war to be free from, the Founding Fathers guaranteed the right to freely report news and circulate opinion without censorship from the government in the First Amendment.

Ever since the ratification of the Bill of Rights, America has, under this definition, had a free press. Instances where this free press has been at work in America are countless, and the Supreme Court of the United States has upheld the right to a free press numerous times.

Our free press shined during the event in history referred to as the Pentagon Papers. The Pentagon Papers referred to a Department of Defense study on US involvement in Vietnam from 1945 to 1967. The study revealed a lot of damning information about the United States' involvement. It showed the US had secretly grown its involvement by bombing Cambodia and Laos, as well as raiding North Vietnam.[10] The papers also revealed the actual reason for the Vietnam War was not to secure an independent, non-communist South Vietnam, but, in the words of Secretary of Defense Robert McNamara, "to contain China." [11]

The papers exposed the US played a key role in helping Ngo Dinh Diem come to power in South Vietnam, then some five

---

10   "Cover Story: Pentagon Papers: The Secret War," *CNN*, June 28, 1971.

11   Ibid.

to ten years later, played a monumental role in supporting the overthrow of Diem.[12] [13]

The Pentagon Papers displayed a vast array of evidence the US government had not been honest with the American public about what it had been doing overseas.

In 1971, Daniel Ellsberg, who had worked on the report, copied large portions of the papers and leaked them to the *New York Times*. The *New York Times* began publishing front-page articles detailing information in the Pentagon Papers on June 13, 1971.[14]

Just a day later on June 14, the *New York Times* received a telegram from the Attorney General of the United States, John W. Mitchell, asking the *New York Times* cease publication of the papers because they were classified and pertained to matters of national security. The telegram read as follows:

"Arthur Ochs Sulzberger President and Publisher The New York Times New York New York

I have been advised by the Secretary of Defense that the material published in The New York Times on

---

12   "Evolution of the War. Counterinsurgency: The Kennedy Commitments and Programs, 1961," in *The Pentagon Papers*, volume 2, pp 1–39. *United States Department of Defense*, distributed by *MountHolyoke*.

13   "The Overthrow of Ngo Dinh Diem, May-November, 1963," in *The Pentagon Papers*, volume 2, pp 201–276. *United States Department of Defense*, distributed by *MountHolyoke*.

14   History.com Editors, "Pentagon Papers," *History*, August 21, 2018.

June 13, 14, 1971, captioned "Key Texts From Pentagon's Vietnam Study" contains information relating to the national defense of the United States and bears a top secret classification.

As such, publication of this information is directly prohibited by the provisions of the Espionage law, Title 18, United States Code, Section 793.

Moreover, further publication of information of this character will cause irreparable injury to the defense interests of the United States.

Accordingly, I respectfully request that you publish no further information of this character and advise me that you have made arrangements for the return of these documents to the Department of Defense.

John W. Mitchell Attorney General" [15]

The *New York Times* refused to cease publication and in response to this, President Richard Nixon and the Attorney General obtained a federal injunction that prevented the *New York Times* from the further publishing of information contained in the Pentagon Papers.[16]

---

15   R. W. Apple Jr., "25 Years Later; Lessons from the Pentagon Papers," *The New York Times,* June 23, 1996.

16   John T. Correll, "The Pentagon Papers," *Air Force Magazine*, February 1, 2007.

The *New York Times* appealed the injunction, and the case moved up the courts and arrived at the Supreme Court just a couple weeks later.

A few days after the injunction, the *Washington Post* followed the *New York Times'* lead and started publishing information contained in the papers themselves. Having been opposed to the *New York Times'* publishing of the Pentagon Papers, it's no surprise the federal government didn't like the *Washington Post* doing the same thing. They sought an injunction to prevent the *Washington Post* from publishing as well, but this time, they weren't able to obtain one. The government appealed this ruling, and the Supreme Court of the United States agreed to hear it jointly with the *New York Times* case as well.

On July 30, 1971, in *New York Times Co. v. United States*, one of the most landmark Supreme Court cases dealing with the free press in America, the Supreme Court sided with the newspapers. In a six-to-three decision, the court ruled the government did not overcome the heavy presumption against prior restraint. [17]

This decision was a big one for the freedom of the press, showing the press in America is free from censorship from the government, exactly what the founders intended.

The free press went to work again during the Watergate scandal.

---

17   "New York Times Company V. United States." *Oyez*, accessed February
       18, 2021.

Watergate refers to the scandal that enveloped President Nixon's presidency and eventually led to his resignation. On June 17, 1972, there was a break-in at the Democratic National Committee headquarters at the Watergate office complex in Washington, DC that Nixon was involved with.[18] For the next two years leading up to his ultimate resignation in August of 1974, Nixon attempted to cover up his involvement in the break-in. However, he ultimately wasn't successful thanks to the work of America's "free" press, most notably the work of two *Washington Post* reporters: Bob Woodward and Carl Bernstein.

Woodward and Bernstein were intrigued by the story and investigated it thoroughly. In "GOP Security Aide Among Those Arrested," they reported one of the burglars, James McCord, was on the payroll of President Nixon's reelection committee.[19]

The two *Washington Post* reporters followed this up by reporting the Grand Jury investigating the burglary had sought testimony from two men who had worked in the Nixon White House.

In "Bug Suspect Got Campaign Funds," Woodward and Bernstein connected the Nixon Campaign to the burglary by reporting one of the burglars had a twenty-five-thou-sand-dollar cashier's check deposited in his bank account.

---

18   "Watergate: The Scandal That Brought down Richard Nixon," *Watergate. info,* accessed February 18, 2021.

19   "Part 1 the Post Investigates," in "The Watergate Story," *The Washington Post,* accessed February 18, 2021.

The check was supposed to be for President Nixon's reelection campaign.[20]

After connecting the Nixon campaign to the burglary of the Democratic National Committee's Headquarters at Watergate, Bernstein and Woodward followed up by breaking a few more stories, including that John Mitchell, the Attorney General of the United States, had controlled and kept secret a fund that paid for the gathering of information on the Democrats.[21] They also reported "that the Watergate bugging incident stemmed from a massive campaign of political spying and sabotage conducted on behalf of President Nixon's reelection and directed by officials of the White House and the Committee for the Reelection of the President."[22]

The Nixon administration tried to cover up the Watergate scandal every step of the way. They criticized the *Washington Post* and tried to intimidate them into stopping their reporting on the scandal. Had it not been for the *Washington Post's* tireless reporting on Watergate, Nixon and his administration may have gotten away with it. This was the "free" press in America working as a check on the government's power.

The freedom the American press has from government censorship was on display in the 1964 Supreme Court case of *New York Times v. Sullivan* as well. This case was between the

---

20 Carl Bernstein and Bob Woodward, "Bug Suspect Got Campaign Funds," *The Washington Post*, August 1, 1972.

21 *The Washington Post*, "Part 1 the Post Investigates."

22 Carl Bernstein and Bob Woodward, "FBI Finds Nixon Aides Sabotaged Democrats," *The Washington Post*, October 10, 1972.

New York Times and L.B. Sullivan, who was a public safety commissioner in Montgomery, Alabama.[23]

The *New York Times* had published an ad from groups protesting the "wave of terror" against Blacks in the South. Sullivan filed suit against the *New York Times* and its four sponsors, claiming the ad defamed him.[24] He claimed multiple untrue remarks caused damages to him and the Montgomery police.[25] The case began in an Alabama court; certain details in the ad were proven to be false, so the trial judge said the statements were libel per se.[26] The jury returned a verdict awarding the full amount requested, five hundred thousand dollars in damages, to Sullivan.[27] The Alabama Supreme Court affirmed this ruling, holding malice could be found in the *New York Times* statements.[28] The *New York Times* then appealed and brought the case to the US Supreme Court.[29]

The question before the Supreme Court was "did the libel law in Alabama infringe on the first amendments freedom of speech and freedom of the press protections?" In a unanimous decision, the Court sided with the *New York Times* and reversed the Alabama Supreme Court's ruling. The Court

---

23 Stephen Wermiel, "New York Times Co. V. Sullivan (1964)," *The First Amendment Encyclopedia,* Middle Tennessee State University.

24 Ibid.

25 Ibid.

26 Ibid.

27 Ibid.

28 Ibid.

29 Ibid.

held when a statement is about a public figure, in order for the press to be liable for libel, it is not enough to simply show the statement is false. It must be made with "actual malice."[30] Actual malice is defined as knowledge the statement was false or reckless disregard for whether or not it was false.

This case was another big win for the "free" press. It ensured the press would have room to make mistakes; therefore, they would still be willing to report on stories and be critical about those in government.

Make no mistake about it, the United States has a press that is free from censorship from the government. It is exactly what the Founding Fathers intended when they drafted the Bill of Rights.

Journalists in the United States have the right to report critical and negative things about their elected officials, and that is more than can be said for some other countries.

So, if America has a press free from censorship from the government, you're probably wondering what the problem is. Isn't that a good thing? You'd be right, it is a good thing the press is free from the government. However, the press is not free from the truly big, powerful interests in this country.

The Founding Fathers wanted the press to act as a fourth estate and be a check on power; they just thought that power

---

30 "New York Times Company V. Sullivan," *Oyez*, accessed February 18, 2021.

would be in the form of the government.[31] They were wrong on that, as the government is just a tool the real powerful people use to express their power. Who are the real unchecked rulers of this country? It's not the government; it's the people with money. The big corporations that bankroll politicians and own the media are the ones who really make the decisions in the United States. There is no check on the power these corporate actors hold.

I am not arguing the press isn't free from government influence; I agree wholeheartedly with that sentiment. I am arguing the press isn't free from the influence of special interests. The reason for this is the system of corporate ownership of the media outlets in the United States. Journalists are free to report critically on elected officials and the government, but it just has to be acceptable by their corporate bosses' standards. Therefore, we do not truly have a "free" press in the United States. The press is not beholden to the people like the Founding Fathers intended; instead, it is beholden to the corporate elites and the elites alone.

---

31   Barron, "No Monument for Madison."

PART 2

CORPORATE OWNERSHIP

CHAPTER 2

CNN

———

There weren't always twenty-four-hour cable news networks in the United States. People used to be required to wait for the evening broadcasts or the morning paper to get their news. It's safe to say, that is far from the case today.

The first twenty-four-hour cable news network in the United States was CNN, or the Cable News Network, Inc. CNN was founded by Ted Turner and Reese Schonfeld in 1980.

In Turner's launch speech back in 1980, he outlined his goals for the network, saying he wished the network's coverage would "bring together in brotherhood and kindness and friendship and in peace the people of this nation and this world."[32]

Well, if I had to weigh in, I'd say that hasn't happened.

---

32 Jeremy Hobson, "How Ted Turner's Vision for CNN Sparked the 24-Hour News Cycle," *wbur*, May 12, 2020.

Turner had been in charge of a local station in Atlanta known as WTBS.[33] It was at this station where he first experimented with all-night coverage and learned people did watch all-night, and the news was what they watched most.[34]

With this knowledge, Turner, along with Schonfeld, launched CNN as a part of the Turner Broadcasting System. On June 1, 1980, they changed the media landscape in this country with their first broadcast. Ever since then, CNN has been on air twenty-four-seven, trying to bring the news to people live as it happens.

CNN struggled to develop its reputation in the broadcast industry at first, but they eventually surpassed the big three networks of NBC, CBS, and ABC. In 1986, CNN was first on the scene when the US space shuttle orbiter Challenger exploded shortly after its launch.[35]

CNN really established itself as a serious player in the TV news industry during the Persian Gulf War, when they were the only network that offered on-scene coverage during the early hours of the coalition bombing campaign. CNN's coverage was displayed by stations and networks around the world.

---

33 David Bravaccio et al., "40 Years of CNN, and the Birth of 24-Hour News Coverage," *Marketplace*, June 19, 2020.

34 Ibid.

35 *Encyclopedia Britannica*, s.v. "CNN," accessed January 19, 2021.

This cemented CNN as the number one TV news network in the United States, and with that came loads of interests from outside companies.

On October 10, 1996, in a 7.5-million-dollar merger, CNN's owner, the Turner Broadcasting System, was acquired by Time Warner, Inc. This deal combined "Time Warner's cable systems, HBO cable channel, the Warner Bros. movie studio, the Time Inc. magazines—including *Time*, *People*, and *Sports Illustrated*—with Turner's Cable News Network, Cartoon Network, Hanna Barbera cartoon studio, Turner Classic Movies, New Line and Castle Rock movie studios, and the Atlanta Braves and Atlanta Hawks pro sports teams."[36]

When one examines the totality of the media conglomerates in our country, it becomes apparent simply providing straight objective news may not be the bottom-line goal of the owners of a cable news network like CNN. They have a lot of other interests as well, and this is just the first of multiple mergers involving CNN's corporate parents.

Time Warner Inc. remained the lead owner of CNN up until 2000, when they merged with AOL, America Online. After the merger, AOL shareholders owned 55 percent of AOL Time Warner for 164 billion dollars.[37] AOL was very successful at the time, which was during the initial Internet boom. The merger was supposed to create a powerhouse, but instead,

36 Thomas S. Mulligan, "Turner-Time Warner Merger Approved by Share-holders," *Los Angeles Times*, October 11, 1996.

37 "M&A Statistics," Institute of Mergers, Acquisitions, and Alliances, accessed January 20, 2021.

it ended up hurting Time Warner because dot-com stocks ultimately tumbled. This led to AOL Time Warner taking big losses. The company eventually dropped AOL from its name altogether and ultimately spun AOL into its own company in 2009.[38]

Time Warner executives decided they needed to downsize their company, so they let their cable division become its own company and separated from Time Inc.[39]

This left Time Warner Inc. owning three major companies: Warner Bros. Entertainment, Inc., The Turner Broadcasting System, and Home Box Office Inc.[40]

Getting back to the point of all of this, CNN was just one small facet of a massive company called Time Warner Inc.

To get to where we stand today, Time Warner was purchased by AT&T. AT&T announced plans to purchase Time Warner for eighty-five billion dollars in 2016.[41] After years of fighting in court with the Department of Justice, the merger was

---

38 "History's Moment in Media: Aol Time Warner Merger," *MediaVillage*, January 14, 2019.

39 Ibid.

40 J. William Carpenter, "3 Major Companies Owned by Time Warner," *Investopedia*, October 14, 2018.

41 Nathan Reiff, "AT&T and Time Warner Merger Case: What You Need to Know," *Investopedia*, updated December 7, 2018.

finally approved in 2018.[42] They dropped the Time Warner brand and changed the name to Warner Media.

Today, AT&T owns Warner Media, which owns what used to be Warner Bros. Entertainment, Inc., The Turner Broadcasting System, and Home Box Office Inc. They have restructured their assets into two divisions: WarnerMedia Entertainment and WarnerMedia News & Sports. CNN is part of WarnerMedia News & Sports.

CNN Ownership Chart

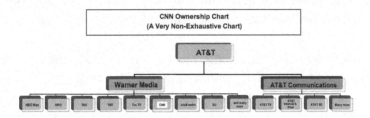

If this is all very confusing to you, that's okay. I think it's pretty confusing for just about everyone. The real point of this is to know CNN is not its own company. It's a TV network that is part of a much larger media conglomeration that has many interests.

---

42   Tony Romm and Brian Fung, "AT&T-Time Warner Merger Approved, Setting the Stage for More Consolidation across Corporate America," *The Washington Post*, June 12, 2018.

Technically speaking, the top dog of CNN is AT&T CEO John T. Stankey, who recently took over for Randall Stephenson.[43] He runs AT&T, who runs WarnerMedia, who runs CNN.

Stankey is estimated to be worth at least 24.8 million dollars. In 2018, Stephenson's compensation from AT&T was twenty-nine million dollars. Twenty-seven-point-three million dollars in stock and other compensation, along with 1.8 million dollars in salary.[44]

These guys calling the shots have a lot of money, and you better believe that influences their decisions on things.

So how does all this connect to the news media in the United States? It's pretty straightforward actually. CNN is owned by corporations, and these corporations are operated by businessmen, successful businessmen at that. What do businessmen like? Why do they do what they do? They like money. They do it for the money. Always follow the money. So, is CNN AT&T's most profitable outlet? Of course, it isn't, but owning a major news network gives them a different form of advantage for their business interests. It helps them influence public opinion and the political directions of our country. They're able to essentially eliminate potential threats to their profits by dismissing them in the "news." In our current

---

43   Aaron Pressman, "Who Is New AT&T CEO John Stankey?," *Fortune*, April 24, 2020.

44   Beth Rifkin, "The 5 Highest Paid Execs in Telecom," *Investopedia*, March 23, 2020.

system, there is nothing that can stop these corporations from doing what they want with the news.

Keith Olbermann, a former anchor at MSNBC, described this phenomenon in an interview with *Rolling Stone* back in 2011.

"It's not about '[The network] is evil,'" Olbermann said. "It's about that media structure—CBS, ABC, CNN, even some of the smaller operations are now multinationals, with these extraordinarily diverse holdings. The corporation is one of the great unheralded human inventions of destruction. It is a way to absolve from any personal liability for a bunch of people. They form together in a massive id and they do whatever they want. In a corporate setting, there's nothing to stop Rupert Murdoch or Disney from doing whatever the hell they want with the news. They could turn it into propaganda for the Chinese government or the socialist party of America, and who's going to stop them?"[45]

Olbermann made a solid point; there is nothing in place to stop them, because we as Americans have been conditioned to believe we have a free press. This notion America has a free press only helps these media conglomerates, because it makes the idea our news would be influenced by someone or some group sound crazy.

The news is free from censorship from the government, so whatever is reported on must be objective and have no agenda, right? It's just the stone-cold truth.

---

45   Mark Binelli, "Keith Olbermann on Why He Left MSNBC – and How He Plans to Get Even," *RollingStone*, June 7, 2011.

That's what these media conglomerates—that consist of the mainstream news outlets like CNN—want you to believe, because it insulates these corporations from the scrutiny they deserve.

The news that comes from CNN and the other mainstream sources is not free from all outside influences. They are not strictly focused on reporting objectively. The truth is the news has an agenda. They don't necessarily care who is president, they just want to make sure candidates who pose a serious threat to their power and profits don't become president or get elected to Congress. They do this through implementing systems of implicit bias in the newsrooms they operate.

The main objective to take away from this chapter is CNN is not an independent network. They are part of a much bigger corporation that has many other interests than just reporting objective facts and being the watchdog or fourth estate the founders intended the press to be.

CHAPTER 3

MSNBC

You're fired! That's what you would hear if you were a producer, anchor, or reporter at MSNBC who dared to report on the fact Comcast is one of the most hated companies in the world.

As David Shuster said, you just don't fuck with the piggy bank, and Comcast is MSNBC's piggy bank.

Now if you thought, well, maybe CNN has some conflicts of interest, but I don't watch CNN, I get my news from MSNBC. Well, I got news for you; MSNBC is eerily similar to CNN when it comes to being a small part of a bigger corporation.

Let's go back to the beginning and track how MSNBC became what it was today. In July of 1996, sixteen years after CNN entered the news industry, the first major competitor to CNN hit the airwaves. As part of a joint venture between Microsoft and the National Broadcasting Company (NBC), the cable news channel MSNBC was launched along with a website, MSNBC.com.[46] NBC was owned by General Electric at the time it launched MSNBC alongside Microsoft. Ever since the beginning of the network, MSNBC has been the offspring of very corporate parents.

In an announcement meeting a year prior to MSNBC's launch, General Electric Chairman Jack Welch, NBC Chairman Bob Wright, and Microsoft Chairman Bill Gates all proclaimed their belief they were creating the future of TV.[47]

"Today, NBC and Microsoft have come together to create news for the next millennium," Wright said. "No network has ever offered news coverage of such breadth and depth before."[48]

"One of the key things is that both of the companies are saying, 'We believe in the world of interactivity, but we're bringing this world into broadcast,'" Gates said. "We'll be working with NBC to create innovative interactive news content and an integrated media experience."[49]

They were talking about providing excellent news, better than ever before, but that wasn't the real reason for their joint venture that was MSNBC. General Electric, one of the biggest corporations in the world at the time, wanted to be aligned with Microsoft, another massive company at the time. This

---

46   Steve Young, "MSNBC Launches Network," *CNNMoney,* July 15, 1996.

47   Variety Staff, "NBC, Microsoft Make News with Joint Venture Cable Web," *Variety,* December 17, 1995.

48   Ibid.

49   Ibid.

wasn't even a secret; they basically admitted to it when they were announcing the establishment of MSNBC.

"Business will be done differently, distribution will be done differently," Welch said. "Who better to hang around with than the company that has done more to change the world than any other?"[50]

MSNBC has been a corporate venture ever since its creation, under the control of some of the biggest, most powerful corporations in the world.

Similar to CNN, MSNBC's corporate parents have changed numerous times through various mergers, but rest assured, they're still owned and operated by large corporate interests. The following is the history of the many mergers that have affected the cable news network MSNBC.

In 1997, NBC merged with Dow Jones & Co to combine their channels outside the United States. It merged NBC's CNBC Europe and Dow Jones' European Business News, NBC's CNBC Asia and Dow Jones' Asia Business News, as well as combined the resources of CNBC and Dow Jones in the US.[51] This merger also resulted in Dow Jones becoming a minority shareholder in MSNBC.[52] In 2001, NBC added another chan-

50   Ibid.

51   "NBC, Dow Jones Reveal Merger Details," *AdAge*, December 10, 1997.

52   Ibid.

nel by purchasing the Telemundo Network for 1.98 billion dollars. [53]

A few years later in 2004, NBC's corporate parent General Electric purchased Vivendi Universal's entertainment assets, including Universal Studios. This deal resulted in the formation of NBC Universal, with General Electric owning 80 percent of the company and Vivendi Universal maintaining a 20 percent stake in the company.[54] The new NBC Universal, with the assets of NBC, in addition to the newly acquired Universal movie and television studios, theme parks, and three cable channels, was estimated to be valued at forty-three billion dollars.[55]

So MSNBC was now a part of a media conglomeration that included big-time movie studios, theme parks, Microsoft, and General Electric. However, in 2005, Microsoft sold a chunk of its shares of MSNBC to NBC Universal, which resulted in NBC Universal holding the controlling interest in MSNBC of 82 percent.[56] However, Microsoft held on to its stake in MSNBC.com.

General Electric maintained its 80 percent ownership stake of NBC Universal up until 2009, when they sold a 51 percent

---

53   Meg James, "NBC to Acquire Telemundo Network for $1.98 Billion," *Los Angeles Times*, October 12, 2001.

54   Bill Carter, "G.E. Finishes Vivendi Deal, Expanding Its Media Assets," *The New York Times*, October 9, 2003.

55   Ibid.

56   Wayne Friedman, "NBC Buys Up More of MSNBC From Microsoft," *MediaPost*, December 27, 2005.

majority stake to Comcast. The terms of the deal required Comcast to pay 6.5 billion dollars upfront and also add 7.25 billion dollars' worth of programming it already owned to NBC Universal. Included in this additional programming were regional sports networks Golf Channel and E! Entertainment Television.[57]

After completing the sale, General Electric used a portion of the cash it received to buy the 20 percent of NBC Universal shares Vivendi still owned.[58]

At this point in time, Comcast was now the majority owner of NBC Universal with a 51 percent stake, and General Electric held the remaining 49 percent of the shares. NBC Universal, which is owned and operated by Comcast, owned MSNBC, the cable news channel, but still shared ownership of MSNBC.com with Microsoft. In 2012, Microsoft sold its stake in the website to Comcast, ending the NBC-Microsoft partnership that was responsible for the launch of MSNBC.[59]

In 2013, Comcast completed its purchase of NBC Universal by buying General Electric's remaining 49 percent share for 16.9 billion dollars, as well as NBC's headquarters at 30 Rockefeller Plaza in New York and CNBC's headquarters in

---

57 David B. Wilkerson and Steve Goldstein, "Comcast Scores Controlling Stake in NBC Universal," *MarketWatch*, December 3, 2009.

58 Ibid.

59 Jeff Blagdon, "Microsoft Sells MSNBC.com Stake to Comcast, Will Launch New MSN News Team," *TheVerge*, July 15, 2012.

Englewood Cliffs, New Jersey, for close to 1.4 billion dollars.[60] In 2016, NBC Universal purchased DreamWorks Animation for 3.8 billion dollars.[61]

At the time of the merger, the Chief Executive of Comcast, Brian Roberts, said the acquisition of NBC Universal was "a perfect fit for Comcast and will allow us to become a leader in the development and distribution of multi-platform 'anytime, anywhere' media that American consumers are demanding."[62]

This shows us the corporation that ultimately controls MSNBC has a main objective that is different from conducting good, honest, wholesome journalism. Comcast is interested in becoming bigger and more profitable, not in MSNBC's viewer knowing the truth about everything that is going on.

This brings us to where things stand today. To recap, the cable news channel MSNBC is owned and operated by NBCUniversal. MSNBC is only one of the many cable networks owned by NBCUniversal. In addition to MSNBC, NBCUniversal owns the following cable networks: Golf Channel, the Olympic Channel, Oxygen, Universal Kids, USA, Sy-FY,

---

60   Ryan Nakashima, "Comcast to Buy GE's 49 Pct Stake in NBCuniversal," *MSN Money*, February 12, 2013, distributed by the Internet Archive Wayback Machine.

61   Brian Fung, "Comcast Is Buying Dreamworks in a $3.8 Billion Acquisition," *The Washington Post*, April 28, 2016.

62   Tim Arango, "G.E. Makes It Official: NBC Will Go to Comcast," *The New York Times*, December 3, 2009.

CNBC, Bravo, E!, and NBC Sports Network.[63] NBCUniversal also owns NBC and Telemundo, and they operate the brands of NBC News and NBC Sports as well.[64] Furthermore, NBCUniversal owns and operates Universal Pictures, Universal Pictures Home Entertainment, DreamWorks, and Focus Features.

This company also has a sizable presence in the world of theme parks and resorts; they own and operate Universal Studios Hollywood, Universal Orlando Resort, Universal Studios Japan, Universal Studios Singapore, and Universal Beijing Resort. They recently launched a streaming service called Peacock in 2020.[65] Sky Group is also a part of NBCUniversal. This is a satellite distribution company in Europe that operates in seven countries and has twenty-four million subscribers.[66] These are just some of the bigger operations NBCUniversal operates, as they also have many local affiliates and own numerous NBC Sports regional sports networks. They also hold a few television production companies.[67]

NBCUniversal is a massive media conglomerate. Its revenues in 2018 were 35.8 billion dollars.[68] However, as previously stated, that's not where the chain of command ends for MSNBC. NBCUniversal is owned by Comcast, which is

---

63   "Brands," *NBCUniversal*, accessed January 17, 2021.

64   Ibid.

65   Ibid.

66   "Sky at a Glance," *Sky,* accessed January 21, 2021.

67   "Brands," *NBCUniversal.*

68   Etan Vlessing, "NBCUniversal Earnings Rise, Management Touts Planned Streaming Service," *The Hollywood Reporter,* January 23, 2019.

a much bigger company. Comcast's annual revenues for 2018, 2019, and 2020 were 94.507 billion dollars, 108.942 billion dollars, and 105.549 billion dollars respectively.[69]

Yeah, Comcast is a big one. In addition to owning NBCUniversal, Comcast also operates the Comcast Cable department, which consists of cable television, broadband Internet, and landline telephone service, operating under the Xfinity brand name.[70] Comcast also owns Comcast Spectacor, which is the parent company of the NHL team the Philadelphia Flyers as well as their home arena, the Wells Fargo Center.[71] They also own Comcast SportsNet, and Comcast has its own venture capital fund, Comcast Ventures, which they use to invest in numerous companies.[72] Some of the businesses in their portfolio include Vimeo, Lyft, and Slack, along with many more.[73]

MSNBC Ownership Chart

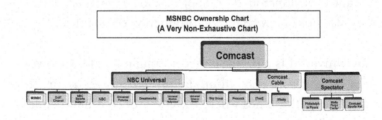

---

69   "Comcast Revenue 2006–2020 | CMCSA," *macrotrends*, accessed January, 20, 2021.

70   "Comcast Corporation CMCSA.O," *Reuters*, accessed January 21, 2021.

71   Sam Carchidi, "Comcast Buying Remaining Flyers Shares from Snider's Estate," *The Philadelphia Inquirer*, September 22, 2016.

72   "Comcast Ventures," *Comcast Ventures*, accessed January 20, 2021.

73   "Portfolio," *Comcast Ventures*, accessed January 20, 2021.

Comcast is a large company with a diverse array of interests. NBCUniversal is just a portion of Comcast, and its news outlets NBC News and MSNBC are even smaller parts. So just like with CNN being only a small portion of AT&T, there are some conflicts of interest when it comes to reporting straight objective hard news on all subjects in this country. You're not going to see very critical news coverage of Comcast on MSNBC, or the big corporate interests they have. For example, they were given the honor of being named *Consumerist*'s "Worst Company in America" twice, in 2010 and 2014.[74] Did that make MSNBC's evening programming? You can bet it didn't. It's simple; MSNBC and NBC won't report on subjects that go against Comcast's interests. You just won't see it, just like you won't see critical coverage of AT&T on CNN.

MSNBC, as well as NBC, are not their own companies. They are not independent. They don't have their own interests and don't call all of the shots for what they put on their airwaves. There is ultimately a chain of command that goes all the way up, from the journalists at these networks to the CEO of Comcast himself, Brian L. Roberts. Roberts isn't involved in day-to-day operations of MSNBC, but I can guarantee you, if MSNBC ever aired a story that was ultra-critical of Comcast or Roberts himself, there would definitely be a reaction, and there would be consequences.

---

74   Adrianne Jeffries, "The Worst Company in America," *The Verge*, August 19, 2014.

CHAPTER 4

FOX NEWS CHANNEL

———

"CNN and MSNBC are nothing but fake news!" Sounds like something former President Trump would say, and he wouldn't be completely wrong.

They definitely aren't 100 percent objective and truthful, that's for sure. Where he was completely wrong was when he would hold up Fox News as being the opposite of MSNBC and CNN, in that they were the ones who were good, honest journalists and reported nothing but the truth. They may talk about different stories, highlight different points of view, and be more favorable to the former president, but Fox News is a lot more similar to CNN and MSNBC than Democrats or Republicans are willing to admit.

All three of them are corporately owned, and that prevents them from being the honest, objective, and reputable news organizations our Founding Fathers intended them to be when they guaranteed the freedom of the press in the Bill of Rights.

Let's examine how Fox News came to be what it is today, and how it, too, is connected to corporate interests.

In order to know what the Fox News Channel is all about, we must first get to know who Rupert Murdoch, the founder of Fox News, was. Murdoch was born and raised in Australia. When his father passed away, he left his twenty-two-year-old son in charge of his newspapers, the *Sunday Mail* and *The News*, based out of Adelaide, Australia.[75] Murdoch took over these papers, and this was the beginning of the construction of the media empire that would one day sprout the Fox News Channel.

Murdoch quickly purchased more papers in Australia. He became the owner of the *Sunday Times* in Perth, Australia, and the *Mirror* in Sydney, Australia.[76] After turning these papers into very successful outlets, he founded Australia's first national daily paper in 1965: the *Australian*.[77] Murdoch eventually moved to London, where he expanded his growing empire by purchasing the Sunday tabloid, *The News of The World*, and another tabloid, *The Sun*.[78] [79]

Murdoch transformed all of his media outlets into super successful institutions by focusing heavily on sex, sports, and crime. It's a strategy he brought with him to the United States when he purchased the *San Antonio News* in 1973. Murdoch

---

75 "Rupert Murdoch Biography," Biography, updated June 29, 2020.

76 Ibid.

77 Ibid.

78 Ibid.

79 Ibid.

then founded *The Star*, a national tabloid, in 1974.[80] He also bought the *New York Post* in 1976.[81] In 1979, Murdoch founded News Corporation (News Corp.), a holdings company for his various media outlets.[82]

Fast forward to 1985 and News Corp. was making big plays. Murdoch purchased a 50 percent share of 20th Century Fox Film for 250 million dollars in March of 1985.[83] That same year, Murdoch and News Corp announced they planned to create a fourth broadcast network to compete with the other three big ones—CBS, ABC, and NBC. News Corp, along with Marvin Davis, who owned the other 50 percent of 20th Century Fox Film, planned to buy six independent TV stations from Metromedia. The channels were WNEW-TV in New York City, WTTG in Washington, DC, KTTV in Los Angeles, KRIV-TV in Houston, WFLD-TV in Chicago, and KRLD-TV in Dallas.[84] Before the deal went through, Murdoch bought Davis out of 20th Century Fox Film by paying him 325 million dollars.[85]

The Metromedia deal was approved and went through in 1986, and later that year, Murdoch expanded his new network's

---

80 Ibid.

81 Ibid.

82 Ibid.

83 Michael Schrage, "Murdoch Agrees to Buy a 50 Percent Share of 20th Century Fox Film," *The Washington Post,* March 21, 1985.

84 "Another Spin for TV's Revolving Door," *Broadcasting,* May 6, 1985, 39–40, via World Radio History.

85 Tim Gray and Pat Saperstein, "Fox Merges with Disney: The Storied Studio's 102-Year History," *Variety,* December 14, 2017.

reach by signing seventy-nine TV stations across the country to affiliation agreements.[86] His Fox Broadcasting Company now had potential coverage of over 80 percent of the country.[87]

As you can see, Murdoch was building a media empire. He had newspapers all over the world, film production studios, and was developing his own network to compete with the big boys. He was fighting to get to the top, and he'd only just begun. He would go on to add much more to his growing media domain.

After signing the local stations to affiliation agreements, Fox was on its way, and it was officially launched in October of 1986.[88] The network saw modest success, but it didn't have its first big hit until it created and aired *The Simpsons* in 1989.[89] This established Fox as a network, but they still weren't considered to be on par with NBC, CBS, and ABC. Murdoch knew this and wanted to solidify his network as one of the big ones. He did this in 1993 when he acquired the television rights to the National Football League's (NFL) National Football Conference (NFC).[90] The NFC was considered to be the most valuable conference of the NFL to hold the rights

---

86 The Associated Press, "New Fox Network Signs up 79 TV Stations across U.S.," *The New York Times*, August 4, 1986.

87 Ibid.

88 Ibid.

89 Gregory Lewis McNamee, "The Simpsons," *Encyclopedia Britannica*, updated August 13, 2020.

90 Bryan Curtis, "The Great NFL Heist: How Fox Paid for and Changed Football Forever," *The Ringer*, December 13, 2018.

to. CBS had the NFC rights and paid 265 million dollars a year for them under its previous deal.[91] They, along with the other two networks, NBC and ABC, didn't want to pay as much as they were paying. CBS offered 250 million dollars a year to renew its rights to the NFC in 1993.[92]

Murdoch saw this as his opportunity to establish Fox as a real competitor to CBS, ABC, and NBC. He viewed the rights to the NFC as if he was buying a network. Murdoch blew the competition out of the water and offered four years for 1.6 billion dollars.[93] The other networks wouldn't match and Fox had its star to build its network around.

In an interview with the Associated Press after Fox secured the rights, Murdoch explained his reasoning for going so big.

"We had pretty clear indications that CBS was prepared to go into the three hundreds," Murdoch said. "We didn't know what that meant though—three hundred ten, three hundred fifty. What? When you start thinking that way, you can get edged out. So, we thought the best thing to do was go to a preemptive strike."[94]

This was a massive play by Murdoch.

---

91   Ibid.

92   Ibid.

93   Ibid.

94   John Nelson, "Rupert Murdoch Earned His Fox Television Network Instant Respe," *The Associated Press*, December 19, 1993.

"This is better than baseball or basketball or a lot of things we'd like to have," Murdoch said. "This is the best. We reached pretty high." [95]

It was Murdoch buying respect for his growing empire.

"Our aim is to be more than just an entertainment network," Murdoch said.[96]

Murdoch set his aim and he would ultimately achieve it. His media conglomerate would only continue to grow after he secured the rights to the NFC.

Ever since going big with the NFL, Fox has been a legit competitor with CBS, ABC, and NBC. Murdoch had his wish, he had a legit broadcast network, and he soon launched the cable channels FX and FX Movie Channel in 1994.[97] News Corp was massive. Murdoch had become a legit media mogul in the United States. However, this was not enough for him.

Murdoch wanted to go in to the TV news industry. He wanted more power.

Murdoch had attempted to purchase CNN, but he lost out to Time Warner.[98] Murdoch then had a falling out with

---

95   Ibid.

96   Ibid.

97   "Our Brands: FX Networks and Productions," *21st Century Fox Careers*, accessed January 20, 2021.

98   Tim Dickinson, "How Roger Ailes Built the Fox News Fear Factory," *RollingStone*, May 25, 2011.

Ted Turner, the founder of CNN and vice chairman and head of Time Warner. This provided motivation to start his own cable news channel to overtake and humiliate Turner's CNN.[99] This twenty-four-hour cable news network Murdoch was going to start was the Fox News Channel. Murdoch wanted his new network to not only outperform CNN; he wanted it to act as a counterweight to what he thought was the "left-wing bias" of CNN.[100]

Murdoch doesn't mince words when talking about his competitors. He would later describe CNN and CNN International as being anti-American.

"The CNN International is a different service, it is even more leftist and anti-American than CNN is," Murdoch said in an interview with the *Financial Times* in 2006. "That's their business, that's fine, but it can't be getting any revenue." [101]

In the same interview, Murdoch would describe how he thought Fox News was balancing the spectrum.

"I mean that [Fox News] has given room to both sides, whereas only one side had it before," Murdoch said.[102]

Murdoch was right, he was giving more airtime to Republicans than CNN, but what he didn't say was most Republican

---

99 James Fallows, "The Age of Murdoch," *The Atlantic*, September 2003.

100 Dickinson, "How Roger Ailes Built the Fox News Fear Factory."

101 "Interview Transcript: Rupert Murdoch and Roger Ailes," *Financial Times*, October 6, 2006.

102 Ibid.

and Democrat politicians are very similar, as they cede to the interests of their wealthy campaign contributors. The right versus left is all for show, because Democrats and Republicans all want the same thing, and that is to maintain the status quo.

Back to the origins of Fox News. Similar to all the wealthy, elite campaign donors in the United States, Murdoch was driven by power and money; he didn't want government regulations imposed by "liberals" to interfere with his plans, and he thought Fox News was the perfect way to ensure this wouldn't happen.[103] So after deciding he was going to start his own cable news channel with a strong right-wing slant, Murdoch started searching for a guy to be in charge of his new project.

The guy he found was Roger Ailes. Ailes had worked in media and conservative politics, and Murdoch found him to be captivating, politically connected, and powerful. Murdoch also liked the fact Ailes also thought the media was inherently biased in favor of Democrats.

Ailes once said, "Bill Clinton has fifteen thousand press secretaries."[104]

Murdoch and Ailes were a perfect match to create the right-wing powerhouse that is Fox News.

---

103 Dickinson, "How Roger Ailes Built the Fox News Fear Factory."
104 Ibid.

Before Fox News made its debut, it already had a large audience. It was one of the requirements Ailes demanded of Murdoch before he agreed to run the network. Typically, content providers, like CNN, charge cable companies for the right to air the programs produced by the content providers. Murdoch and Fox News did things a different way in the beginning. They paid the cable companies to air it. In order to get Fox News into twenty-five million homes, Murdoch paid cable companies as much as twenty dollars a subscriber.[105] This strategy made sure Fox News would have a massive audience before any content was even aired. It started with a large audience, and its audience has only continued to grow.

Today, Fox News is the most watched cable news channel in the United States. It has been ever since they overtook CNN for the top spot in 2002.[106] Not only is Fox News the most dominant cable news channel, but it has also become one of the most watched networks throughout all of cable television. In January 2019, Fox News placed second in average prime-time audience of 2.2 million viewers. The first-place network was ESPN, but their numbers were inflated because of the NFL playoffs and college football.[107] The sheer size of Fox News' audience gives it a vast amount of power.

Murdoch and Ailes built an absolute powerhouse of a cable news network in the Fox News Channel. The network

---

105 Ibid.

106 Mark Joyella, "Fox News Marks 17 Years at No. 1, but MSNBC's Rachel Maddow Beats Sean Hannity," *Forbes*, January 29, 1998.

107 Ibid.

brought in 816 million dollars in estimated profit in 2010.[108] But just like its competitors CNN and MSNBC, Fox News is just a small part of a much bigger company, and it has an agenda because of that. Fox News' bias may be more obvious, but it is the same as MSNBC and CNN. They don't report on things that could threaten the interests of big businesses, because they are owned and operated by, you guessed it, big businesses.

To sum everything up, the Fox News Channel is a part of Rupert Murdoch's much larger media empire. Murdoch founded News Corporation in 1979, which he used as a holdings company for his various media assets. In 2013, he split the company into two companies; one retained the name News Corp. and the other was named 21st Century Fox.[109] News Corp. retained Murdoch's publishing companies, such as the *New York Post* and the *Wall Street Journal*, whereas 21st Century Fox was made up of the movie and TV divisions, including the notable brands of 20th Century Fox, the Fox Broadcast Network, Fox Sports, and Fox News.[110] Murdoch remained in control of both of these companies.

In 2017, Murdoch decided to sell many of 21st Century Fox's assets. 21st Century Fox's assets of the Fox Broadcasting Company, Fox News, Fox Business Network, and the Fox Sports national operations of Fox Sports 1, Fox Sports 2, and the Big Ten Network were spun off into a new company

---

108 Dickinson, "How Roger Ailes Built the Fox News Fear Factory."

109 "News Corp Officially Splits in Two," *BBC*, June 28, 2013.

110 AP, "News Corp Formally Splits in Two," *USA Today*, updated June 28, 2013.

named Fox Corporation. The rest of 21st Century Fox was sold to the Walt Disney Company for 52.4 billion dollars.[111]

That's a big number, 52.4 billion dollars. It goes to show just how much money there is in TV, and when there's billion-dollar sums of money up for grabs, you know that will have an impact on how their stations operate.

Rodger Ailes once described the TV business as a license for printing money.[112]

Today, Murdoch, along with his sons, still owns both Fox Corp and News Corp.

Fox News Channel Ownership Chart

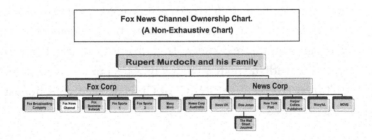

Fox News has been part of a much bigger corporate machine since its inception in 1996. It has always been subjected to the interests of its parent companies and, ultimately, Rupert

---

111 "The Walt Disney Company to Acquire Twenty-First Century Fox, Inc., after Spinoff of Certain Businesses, for $52.4 Billion in Stock," The Walt Disney Company, December 14, 2017.

112 *Financial Times*, "Interview Transcript."

Murdoch. Roger Ailes played a large role in the day-to-day operations and growing Fox News into what we know it as today, but ultimately, the reason for Fox News' creation was Murdoch, his media empire, and his desire to influence the politics of this country.

Fox News has always been favorable to the right side of the political spectrum in the United States. That's obvious, and it can be said MSNBC or CNN are more favorable to the Democrats who are in line with the interests of big business. These networks may appear to be different due to their stances on social issues, but they are still extremely similar in the fact they favor the interests of big business and aren't the objective, hard-hitting, fact-based news outlets that were envisioned by our Founding Fathers when they were drafting the Bill of Rights. The reason for this is they aren't independent. They aren't free. Sure, they are free from the government, but they aren't free from the interests of their corporate billionaire owners. This means they aren't free to report the truth, no matter what it may be. For this reason, we can't treat Fox News, MSNBC, or CNN as reputable, honest news networks.

The three big cable news outlets in this country are all extremely similar in how they are owned and operated. The way this system of corporate ownership makes its impact is the same with all of them, and we will discuss that in the coming chapters.

CHAPTER 5

THE BROADCAST NETWORKS & THE NEWSPAPERS

———

THE BROADCAST NETWORKS

"Counting down to the premiere of *Star Wars: The Rise of Skywalker*, it hits theaters Friday. We can't wait, can we, guys? I can't sleep at night."[113]

These were the words expressed on ABC's *Good Morning America* in the week leading up to the premiere of the film *Star Wars: The Rise of Skywalker*. No harm in a few hosts talking about a movie, right? Well, this is actually one of the most blatant examples of business interests impacting news content. *Star Wars: The Rise of Skywalker* is a Lucas Film production, and Lucas Film is ultimately owned by the Walt

———

113 Good Morning America, "Countdown to 'Star Wars: The Rise of Sky-walker,'" *ABCNEWS*, December 15, 2019, video, 3:36.

Disney Company. What else does the Walt Disney Company own, you ask? Well, they own a lot of things, including ABC.

Disney uses their news programs, like *Good Morning America*, to promote its business interests, like the premiere of *Star Wars: The Rise of Skywalker*. This may not be so bad if competing companies were able to air advertising on ABC as well, but they aren't. Disney bans competitors from advertising on their networks. They banned Netflix from advertising on all of their channels, except for ESPN.[114] This is a great conflict of interest and goes to show when a network is owned by a bigger company, the owner's interests always have an impact on that network's content.

So, if you were ever wondering if the broadcast networks were any better than the cable news channels, sadly, the answer is no, not really. Yep, they are corporately owned as well. The broadcast networks I'm referring to are the big ones. They are NBC, CBS, ABC, and Fox.

We've already discussed NBC and Fox to certain extents when talking about MSNBC and Fox News, so I will be brief in assessing their corporate ties.

Just like MSNBC, NBC is owned and operated by NBCUniversal, which is a subsidiary of Comcast. With this being true, the news teams at NBC and MSNBC respectively are subject to the same incentive structure: a structure that incentives being friendly to corporate America. Really, MSNBC and

114 Todd Haselton, "Disney Bans Netflix Ads from All of Its TV Channels except ESPN," *CNBC*, October 4, 2019.

NBC News are essentially the same things, just on different channels on your TV. The hindrances that come from corporate ownership that affect MSNBC, affect NBC News just as much.

NBC Ownership Chart

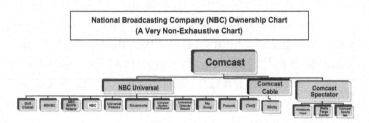

Similar to how NBC and MSNBC are under the same corporate umbrella, FOX is under the same corporate umbrella as the Fox News Channel. FOX is a part of Rupert Murdoch's empire and therefore, its news programs have the same obstacles to being objective as does the content airing on the Fox News Channel.

FOX Ownership Chart

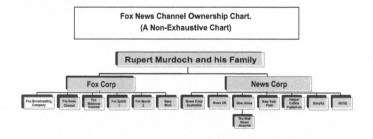

Now we can expand our focus to more American companies when talking about ABC and CBS. First, let's take a look at CBS.

CBS, or the Columbia Broadcasting System, began as a radio network in the late 1920s.[115] In 1931, CBS aired the first regularly scheduled television broadcasting in the country on experimental station W2XAB in New York City. CBS was broadcasting seven hours a day, seven days a week by the end of the year.[116] Fast forward to 1952, and CBS launched a division called CBS Films.[117] This division's name was eventually changed to Viacom. In 1971, Viacom separated from CBS and became its own company.[118]

The two separate companies, CBS and Viacom, were eventually both purchased by other companies. In 1987, Viacom was acquired by National Amusements, a movie theater company.[119] CBS, on the other hand, was purchased by Westinghouse Electric Corporation for 5.4 billion dollars in 1995.[120] The new company was renamed the CBS Cor-

---

115 John F. Schneider, "Remembering CBS Radio's Beginnings," *RADIO-WORLD*, updated July 15, 2020.

116 "CBS At 75 Feature: CBS Timeline of Milestones," *ViacomCBS Press Express*, October 23, 2003.

117 Jude Brennan, "CBS Films' Presidency: And Then There Was One," *Forbes*, July 23, 2014.

118 "Viacom Inc. History," *Funding Universe*, accessed January 20, 2021.

119 "National Amusements Inc. History," *Funding Universe*, accessed January 20, 2021.

120 Sallie Hofmeister and Jane Hall, "CBS Agrees to Buyout Bid by Westinghouse : Entertainment: $5.4-Billion Merger Would Create Biggest TV,

poration. Both of these new companies continued to grow and made numerous other acquisitions. In 1999, National Amusement's Viacom purchased the company that birthed them in the first place. Viacom acquired CBS Corporation for 35.6 billion dollars.[121] In 2005, the company split back into two companies, CBS Corporation and Viacom Inc.[122] They were both still owned by National Amusements. This split didn't last long, as the two merged back together in 2019 to form ViacomCBS Inc.[123]

This is where things stand today. ViacomCBS is controlled by National Amusements, Inc. National Amusements is a family business that is run by the Redstone family. Founded by Michael Redstone in 1936, it was then passed to his son Sumner Redstone. Sumner passed away on August 11, 2020, so his daughter Shari Redstone now controls the company.[124] *Forbes* had Sumnar Redstone's net worth at 2.6 billion dollars as of April 2020.[125]

ViacomCBS's current brands include BET, CBS News, CBS Sports, Comedy Central, MTV, Nickelodeon, Showtime,

Radio Empire. But the Deal Faces Obstacles.," *Los Angeles Times*, August 2, 1995.

121 M. Corey Goldman and Tom Johnson, "Viacom Tunes in to CBS," *CNNMoney*, September 7, 1999.

122 CBS/AP, "CBS, Viacom Formally Split," *CBSNEWS*, January 3, 2006.

123 Jonathan Berr, "Here Is Everything You Need to Know about the Viacom-CBS Merger," *Forbes*, November 26, 2019.

124 Alex Sherman, "Sumner Redstone Handed a Media Empire to His Daughter, Shari, Who Now Controls Its Fate," *CNBC*, updated August 12, 2020.

125 "#804 Sumner Redstone," *Forbes*, accessed January 20, 2021.

Paramount, Paramount Television Studios, CBS Sports Network, and many more.[126] Just look at their website; ViacomCBS is a big company.

So, there you have it, another mainstream news source in the US that isn't independent from corporate interests. CBS News is part of a much larger company, and ultimately owned by a billionaire family.

CBS Ownership Chart

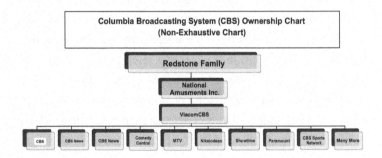

On to ABC, the American Broadcasting Company, or the alphabet network as some call it. ABC was established as a radio network in 1943 after the NBC Blue Network was purchased by Edward J. Noble.[127] In order to keep up with their competition, the new ABC eventually added TV to their portfolio of operations in 1948.[128] The company saw its first big merger when United Paramount Companies, a movie

---

126 "Making Connections around the World," *ViacomCBS*, accessed January 21, 2021.

127 "History Timeline of ABC," *NoCable*, accessed January 21, 2021.

128 Ibid.

theater company, purchased ABC for twenty-five million dollars in shares.[129]

The company was referred to as American Broadcasting Paramount Theaters, until it was renamed the American Broadcasting Companies in 1965.[130] ABC had continued to grow and had been approached by numerous companies with merger offers. General Electric, then owner of NBC, was one of them.[131] (It's crazy how connected all this is.) ABC eventually agreed to a merger with International Telephone and Telegraph in 1965. However, the deal never went through because the US Department of Justice was concerned about how overseas ownership could influence the journalistic integrity of ABC.[132] [133]

This is pretty ironic since being owned by big companies here at home in the US definitely seems to influences journalistic integrity as well.

Continuing on, ABC was purchased by Capital Cities Communications in 1985 for 3.5 billion dollars.[134] The new company was then called Capital Cities/ABC Inc. up until it accepted another merger, but this time from the Walt Disney Company.

---

129 Ibid.

130 Ibid.

131 *New World Encyclopedia,* s.v. "American Broadcasting Company," accessed January 21, 2021.

132 Ibid.

133 "History Timeline of ABC," *NoCable.*

134 Ibid.

The Walt Disney Company purchased Capital Cities/ABC Inc. for nineteen billion dollars in 1995.[135] Walt Disney has acquired other assets, merged them with ABC, and restructured its divisions every now and then, but this pretty much brings us up-to-date on the ownership of ABC.

ABC is owned by the Walt Disney Company. Along with ABC, Walt Disney owns hundreds of companies, including ESPN, Touchstone Pictures, Marvel, Lucas Film, Pixar, The History Channel, 21st Century Fox (they purchased this from Rupert Murdoch, who we all know by now), Disney Channel, Disneyland, and many, many, more.[136]

Here's a chart to show all the businesses that make up The Walt Disney Company.

ABC Ownership Chart

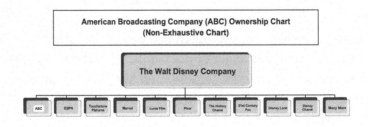

So yeah, ABC News is most certainly not an independent organization.

---

135 Ibid.

136 Carly Hallman, "Every Company Disney Owns: A Map of Disney's Worldwide Assets," *TitleMax*, accessed January 21, 2021.

THE NEWSPAPERS

The newspapers, once our nation's gold standard, simply aren't much better than our TV news, since they are corporately owned as well. I will give them the credit of not having been bought and sold as many times as the networks and cable channels, but there is certainly still a corporate structure.

The *New York Times* is probably the best of the bunch when it comes to the mainstream papers. It is owned and operated by the New York Times Company, a holding company started by Adolph Ochs in 1896. Ochs became the publisher of the paper when he and a group of investors bought it in 1896.[137] The paper has remained in the Ochs-Sulzberger family having been passed down from generation to generation.

Today the *New York Times* has a dual Class share structure. They have publicly traded Class A shares and privately held Class B shares.[138] The Ochs-Sulzberger family possesses a controlling interest in the Class B shares, which affords them 70 percent of the company's board.[139] A. G. Sulzberger is the current publisher of the *New York Times*. He is paid millions of dollars per year, so just because he isn't the richest guy

---

137 "The New York Times Company History," *Funding Universe*, accessed January 20, 2021.

138 Catherine Clifford, "Tech Billionaires from Bezos to Benioff Are Buying Media Companies, but 'New York Times Is Not for Sale,'" *CNBC Make It,* updated November 8, 2018.

139 Ibid.

in the world, doesn't mean there aren't conflicts of interest there.[140]

New York Times Ownership Chart

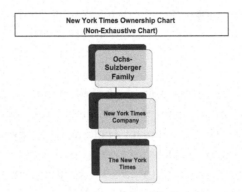

Sulzberger may not be the richest guy in the world, but Jeff Bezos was. Bezos, as of January 21, 2021, had a net worth of 192.3 billion dollars.[141] He's the second richest guy in the world and the founder, former CEO, current chair of the Amazon board, and president of Amazon. He was the richest guy in the world up until Elon Musk, CEO and co-founder of Tesla, surpassed him for the title of richest man in the world in January 2021 with an estimated 197 billion dollars. The two billionaires can oscillate between richest and second richest man in the world, depending on how their respective companies' stocks are trading on a given day.[142] The point is Jeff Bezos is one of the wealthiest two men in the world. By being one of the richest men in the world, Bezos is afforded

140 "Arthur Sulzberger Net Worth," *wallmine,* updated January 1, 2021.

141 "#1 Jeff Bezos," *Forbes,* January 21, 2021.

142 Dan Moskowitz, "The 10 Richest People in the World," *Investopedia*, updated January 25, 2021.

the luxury of essentially being able to buy anything in the world, and among his many purchases is the *Washington Post*.

That's right, one of the richest men in the world owns one of our nation's most reputable newspapers. This screams conflict of interest.

Bezos purchased the *Washington Post* from the Washington Post Company in 2013 for two hundred fifty million dollars in cash.[143] The paper had been owned by the Meyer-Graham family since 1933.[144]

The *Washington Post* is one of the many assets Jeff Bezos owns. He owns Amazon, Blue Origin Rocket Company, Nash Holdings (the holding company that owns Washington Post), Bezos Expeditions, and the Bezos Family Foundation.[145] Through Bezos Expeditions, he owns stakes in companies such as Airbnb, Business Insider, Twitter, Uber, and many more.[146] Simply put, the *Washington Post* is not independent. It may be the most corrupt of all the mainstream media sources out there. It's sad because it has such a great history of strong journalism with the Watergate coverage and the publishing of the Pentagon Papers, but being purchased by Jeff Bezos threw all that out the window.

143 Paul Farhi, "Washington Post to Be Sold to Jeff Bezos, the Founder of Amazon," *The Washington Post,* August 5, 2013.

144 Chalmers M. Roberts, "Eugene Meyer Bought Post 50 Years Ago," *The Washington Post,* June 1, 1983.

145 Megan Henney, "A Look at Jeff Bezos' Biggest Assets," *FOXBusiness,* April 4, 2019.

146 "Bezos Expeditions," *Bezos Expeditions,* accessed January 21, 2021.

The Washington Post Ownership Chart

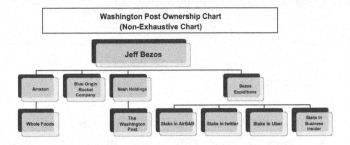

Other big papers, such as the *Wall Street Journal* and the *New York Post*, are also corporately owned. Both of these papers are part of Rupert Murdoch's News Corp.[147] The point is these aren't independent either.

The Wall Street Journal Ownership Chart

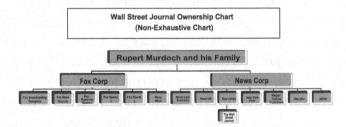

The New York Post Ownership Chart

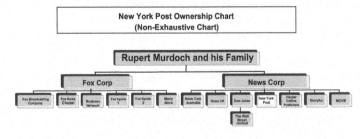

---

147 "About Us," *NewsCorp*, accessed January 21, 2021.

All of the mainstream news outlets in this country have undeniable ties to corporate America. Whether it be the big three cable news channels of CNN, MSNBC, and the Fox News Channel; the broadcast networks of NBC, CBS, ABC, and Fox; or the big national papers like the *New York Times*, *Washington Post*, *Wall Street Journal*, and *New York Post*; they are all owned by big businesses and, in turn, big businessmen who have a lot of money and want more of it. This prevents us as Americans from receiving the good, thorough, complete, objective, wholesome, and honest journalism we deserve.

Now, if you ask someone who is currently working in the mainstream media if their owners impact their coverage, they will be offended and say of course not, they are independent and dedicated to high-quality journalism; but that simply isn't true. They're either straight up lying, or they simply don't know they aren't free to report what they want. Michael Parenti, a political scientist and author of many books, including *Inventing Reality: The Politics of News Media*, described this phenomenon perfectly in one of his many lectures.

He said most of the reporters who were giving him stories about censorship and top-down control were all ex-reporters, and the ones still working didn't agree.[148]

"The ones who are still in there absolutely vehemently deny that there is any such thing like this," Parenti said. "They get very indignant. They say: 'Are you telling me I'm not my own man? I'll have you know that in seventeen years with

---

148 Michael Parenti, "Inventing Reality," accessed January 21, 2021.

this paper I always say what I like.' And I say to them: 'You say what you like, because they like what you say.'" [149]

"I mean, you don't know you're wearing a leash if you sit by the peg all day. It's only if you start to wander to a prohibited perimeter that you feel the tug, you see. So, you're free because your ideological perspective is congruent with that of your boss. So you have no sensation of being at odds with your boss." [150]

This describes the system of corporate ownership and how its effects can be invisible to some who are caught up in it, but they are in fact there. There are many problems with this structure, and I will lay them out and how we can fix them in the next two sections. When talking about the news in America, things aren't as black and white as the guy at the top of the chain telling the reporter what to say, but the system effectively works like that.

Hell, take it from Rupert Murdoch himself, who once said, "The buck stops with the guy who signs the checks." [151]

---

149 Ibid.

150 Ibid.

151 "'The Buck Stops with the Guy Who Signs the Checks,'" *inspiringquotes. us,* accessed January 21, 2021.

PART 3

THE SYSTEM AT WORK

The mainstream media in this country is not made up of various independent journalistic outlets. We know that, so why is it a problem? How is this the root of the problems with the news in the United States?

The answer to this is simple, yet not simple at the same time. Each outlet has its agenda that stems from its corporate ownership. They may vary a bit between outlets, but for the most part, they all are extremely similar. Fox News is more openly conservative on social issues, like race, sexuality, gender, etc., than MSNBC or CNN, but they are all overwhelmingly similar in their desire for business-friendly politics and lust to maintain the status quo.

They don't care about the average American working paycheck to paycheck; they don't care about the people of Flint, Michigan, who were without clean drinking water for years; they don't care about the individuals losing their jobs due to economic restructuring.[152] All they want is what is best for the financial elites of this country, or in other words, the people and corporations who own them.

So, this is the obvious and simple part, but how this agenda makes its impact is a little more hidden. It's not as simple as a Comcast executive walking into the MSNBC studios and telling Chuck Todd, Rachel Maddow, and the other hosts to make sure they give easy softball questions to Pete Buttigieg or Joe Biden while crucifying Bernie Sanders and getting Andrew Yang's name wrong.[153]

The system doesn't work like that; instead, journalists either get the message through subtle hints, or they don't advance in their career. The system filters out the ideas it doesn't want to become mainstream. If you're a journalist at MSNBC and you are critical of establishment Democrats, you won't be in line for promotions and may just lose your job outright. If you're at Fox News and you swim in the direction the company wants you to, you will move up and be featured in bigger roles.

---

152 Melissa Denchak, "Flint Water Crisis: Everything You Need to Know," *NRDC*, November 8, 2018.

153 Nicholas Wu, "'John Yang?' Andrew Yang Pokes Fun at MSNBC for Flubbing His Name in Broadcast," *USA Today*, September 10, 2019.

Once journalists become aware of this phenomenon, they have a choice to make. They can either do what is asked of them, or they can be the idealistic journalist they wanted to be at the beginning of their careers. If they choose the latter, they will typically find themselves out of a job.

This systemic filtration leads to newsrooms across the major networks and papers being filled with journalists who all share the same point of view. For the journalists who don't share the same view and happen to make it through this filtration of sorts, they are faced with the overwhelming pressure to conform and go with the majority's idea or view. It creates a bubble that is insulated from the rest of America. This leads to the news being what it is today: very slanted, lacking diversity of perspectives, and outright missing a lot of issues facing everyday Americans.

This section will outline how this system works and the effects it has on American life.

CHAPTER 6

WHO'S IN THE NEWSROOM PART 1

Newsrooms in America lack diversity.

Sure, there is diversity based on race, gender, and sexual orientation in the mainstream media. CNN's Don Lemon, NBC News' Lester Holt, and MSNBC's Joy-Ann Reid are all prominent African-American news anchors. Rachel Maddow of MSNBC and Don Lemon and Anderson Cooper of CNN are all members of the LGBTQ community, who host prime-time shows on the major cable news networks. There are many female hosts, including the likes of MSNBC's Rachel Maddow, Joy Reid, and Nicole Wallace, CNN's Kate Bolduan and Erin Burnett, as well as Fox News' Dana Perino and Laura Ingraham. This diversity is great and there should be more of it. It certainly helps in terms of trying to get more viewpoints in the media.

However, even with this diversity, the American mainstream media is severely lacking when it comes to diversity in perspectives. The reason for this is in order to get to the positions these prominent journalists hold, they had to play ball. They had to stick to the party line and not stray from what their corporate bosses wanted them to do. The people who did this have gone on to have very successful careers in the mainstream media; the others, well, they weren't so lucky.

David Shuster, a current on-air contributor for *Quick Hits*, has been a journalist for quite some time now. He's been around the block and worked at all three of the big cable news networks in the United States: CNN, Fox News, and MSNBC. Having worked in the industry for so long and at so many different places, Shuster has a substantial understanding of the underlying system that controls the industry and how it incentivizes certain perspectives to rise above others. I talked to Shuster and he summed up the dynamics nicely.

"There is an awareness that all the journalists, all the talent, and I'm not talking about entry-level people, but people who have been around, who are smart, and who have been in the business for a few years, and might be in a position to be a top-level correspondent or host their own show, they are abundantly aware, they are made aware of where the channel or the network organization's priorities are," Shuster said. "It is made clear to them, don't fuck with the piggy bank, or the people who are buttering your bread."

This one quote really conceptualizes the whole problem with our media right now. Journalists are handicapped in the fashion they can't follow the truth to wherever it takes them. They have to stay in line and go with the overall agenda of their respective network.

Shuster worked for the Fox News Channel from 1996 to 2002.[154] He shared a story from his time there about one of his fellow reporters facing this exact dilemma we are talking about: to report the truth or to do what his bosses want and not report the truth. This story is a perfect example because this guy made his decision and has been rewarded handsomely for it. He is now one of the lead anchors at the Fox News Channel: Bret Baier.

It really illustrates how journalists will stray from their duties of reporting the truth to satisfy their network bosses.

Back in 2000, right after the presidential election, when Florida was still being contested between Al Gore and George W. Bush, Fox News was pushing a narrative Bush would have won Florida had republican voters not been disenfranchised.

The theory made some sense at first. It was said on election day the networks called Florida for Gore before all the polls closed and because of that, Republican voters who were in line and hadn't voted yet went home.

How did this happen? Well, Florida spans over two time zones, most of the state is in the Eastern time zone, but the northern panhandle stretches into the Central Standard time zone. The panhandle is home to more Republican voters than the rest of the state. Polls across the state closed at 7:00 p.m.,

---

154 David Shuster, "David Shuster," Linkedin, accessed January 25, 2021.

but because the panhandle stretched into the Central time zone, polls there were technically open until 8:00 p.m. Eastern time. When the polls in the Eastern time zone closed at 7:00 p.m. Eastern Time, networks called Florida for Vice President Al Gore; however, the polling locations in the Central time zone were still open.

So, the thousands of people still in line to vote in the panhandle, a lot of them Republicans, went home once they heard Gore won, because why would someone wait in line for an hour to cast a vote that didn't matter. Republican turnout and support for George W. Bush was suppressed because of the early call for Gore, and had it not happened, Bush would have won. This is what Fox News, other conservative outlets, and conservatives in general were saying.

It sounds plausible. The state shouldn't have been called before all the polling locations were closed and everyone voted. If this was in fact the case, surely, it'd be easy to find Republicans who went home, right? Well, this brings us back to Shuster's story.

Shuster was working as a reporter for Fox News at the time. He said a fellow reporter was assigned this story and was sent out to find people who went home without voting because of the premature call of Al Gore winning Florida. This reporter went out and talked to voters in the panhandle and according to Shuster, the guy didn't find one person who went home early.

Shuster told me, "It was a pretty good theory at the beginning, and it was certainly worth exploring. So, as soon as the

Florida recount started, I was sent to Tallahassee to cover the capital there and the recount stuff.

"Bret Baier, who's now the main anchor at Fox News, was an up-and-coming correspondent at the time. He was based out of the Atlanta Bureau for Fox News, and he was sent to the panhandle to find all of these thousands of Republicans who were disenfranchised because the networks called Florida for Gore initially.

"I remember him showing up in Tallahassee after he had been in the Florida Panhandle for a couple of days.

"I said, 'Oh Bret, how's your story going?'

"He said something to the effect of, 'I couldn't find a single person who left the line or decided not to vote because of anything the networks did in the final hour before the panhandle closed.'

"I then said, 'Oh okay, so Bret, you're going to do that story, right, because we still have people every hour of every day on Fox News saying 'George W. Bush would have won Florida. He would have won Florida if it hadn't been for the networks disenfranchising those voters.' I said, 'Bret, you're going to do this story though because Fox keeps repeating the narrative, and it's not true.'

"Bret said, 'No, I'm not going to do the story.'

"I said, 'Why not?'

"He said something like, 'Because it's clear that Fox News wants this talking point out there and it's not my responsibility to try and correct them.'

"I said, 'No, it is your responsibility. You're a journalist, you were assigned to this story, you should report what you found, if you found that this story doesn't exist.'

"And Bret said, 'I'm not going to do that.'"

Shuster said what Baier found completely contradicted what Fox and other conservative outlets were saying. He said he tried to convince Baier to do the story, but he couldn't change his mind.

Shuster told me it was at that moment he thought, wow, this guy is going to go pretty far here at Fox News.

It turns out Shuster was on the right track. For those of you who don't know who Bret Baier is, he is currently the host of *Special Report with Bret Baier* on the Fox News Channel. He is also the chief political correspondent for Fox. So yeah, one wouldn't be wrong to say Baier has carved out a nice little career for himself at Fox News.[155]

Why has Baier been so successful in his rise up the ranks of Fox News? It's because he hasn't "fucked with the piggy bank," as Shuster would say. He does what his bosses want him to do, even when it involves not telling the objective truth. He's

---

155 "Bret Baier," *Bret Baier*, accessed January 25, 2021.

made the decision to go in the direction his bosses want him to go, and he has been rewarded handsomely for doing so.

This story displays the choices journalists are faced with daily. Had Baier done the opposite of what he did, had he gone against the network's wishes, he most likely wouldn't be where he is today, and that is a sad reality.

CHAPTER 6

WHO'S IN THE NEWSROOM PART 2

The pressure to conform to the network's agenda is present at all the mainstream media outlets. The journalists who conform, like Bret Baier, rise up in the ranks and have successful careers. Their voices get amplified in the process, and in turn, the outlets' corporate owners get their desired message in the "news." On the other hand, if a journalist doesn't conform, they will be demoted or let go completely.

Cenk Uygur, the founder of independent media outlet The Young Turks Network (TYT Network) and cohost of its flagship program *The Young Turks* (TYT), is a perfect example of what happens at the mainstream media outlets when you don't comply with your boss's orders.

Uygur had started TYT as a progressive talk radio show on Sirius Satellite Radio in 2002.[156] Four years later in 2006, TYT became the first online streaming daily talk show after Uygur turned down a two-hundred-fifty-thousand-dollar radio-only deal.[157] The audience grew rapidly. By February of 2010, *The Young Turks* had more than two hundred million views on YouTube.[158]

So when MSNBC had an opening for a new host in 2010, Uygur used his massive audience to launch him to the top of the list.

"MSNBC was looking for a new host and I decided to do something crazy," Uygur told me. "I announced my candidacy for the host position, and nobody ever does that. My agent was mortified, and he said, 'You're never going to get it that way.' I was like, 'I'm never gonna get it the other way; I'm an online host, it's not like they are going to come to find me.' So, our fans sent thousands of e-mails and messages and pictures to MSNBC, and it was so effective that I got a meeting. In fact, I got two meetings and those went well, and I don't really know, but they certainly had an effect. They were there like, 'Oh okay, I get it. This guy's really popular. This might work.'"

Uygur didn't get his shot to shine on MSNBC until MSNBC host Dylan Rattigan needed a sub and wanted it to be Uygur.

---

156 Chavala Madlena, "Cenk Uygur on the Success of the Young Turks," *The Guardian*, April 26, 2010.

157 Ibid.

158 Ibid.

"Ultimately it was Dylan Rattigan who insisted that I sub in for him when he went on 4th of July break," Uygur said. "That was my big break and the first time I got on. It must have been 4th of July weekend—not weekend, like that Friday in 2010."

Uygur subbed for Rattigan.

"At that point, it went exceedingly well," Uygur told me. "I didn't have any context when they came to tell me the ratings; I was like, 'Okay, is that good?' They said, 'Yeah, you're doing better than Dylan.' So no knock on Dylan, he's doing great, but that's crazy. That never happens.'

"And when [you get good ratings], what they do is try you more, right," Uygur said. "If you had ratings that sucked, they wouldn't have tried you again. So, then I started subbing in for all sorts of hosts—Ed Schultz, Keith Olbermann, etc.

"And that went great. I was beating nearly every host I subbed in for, and that's just unprecedented. That has a lot less to do with me than it does with our audience [TYT's audience]. Our audience [TYT's audience] is spectacular.

"[MSNBC] was like 'Whoa,' so then they said, 'Okay, look, let's try you out here and give you the three o'clock hour for like a month as a test.'"

That's exactly what happened and Uygur did very well. He had great ratings, and when Keith Olbermann departed

MSNBC in January of 2011, Cenk Uygur took over the 6:00 Eastern Time slot.[159]

Uygur held this position and did well with it until July of 2011, when he and MSNBC went their separate ways.[160]

What led to Uygur's departure is what is really interesting and is a perfect example of the pressure journalists are under to conform to the views of their owners.

"So, then a series of things happened," Uygur said. "In March, Phil Griffin calls me to his office. It was March or April and he said, 'Hey Cenk, I was just in DC and they're not happy with your tone.' So, he never clarified who in Washington was not happy with my tone, but he then had this funny crazy story that he told me about how outsiders are cool and they wear leather jackets and ride motorcycles, but at NBC, we're not outsiders, we're insiders, and you got to start acting like it."

Uygur followed this up by saying it was easy to remember because it wasn't a normal speech.

"I was like, 'Wow, this is the speech,'" Uygur told me. "I didn't think this speech existed. I thought it was all subtle, but Phil's not known for subtly. So, he just flat out said it.

---

159 Rebecca Ford, "Cenk Uygur Tells Keith Olbermann That MSNBC Trades Truth for Access (Video)," *The Hollywood Reporter*, July 22, 2011.

160 David Lieberman, "'Young Turks' Cenk Uygur Out at MSNBC," *Deadline*, July 20, 2011.

"And so it's clear that what he wanted me to do was ease up on Obama and the Democrats. I had had a former Republican congressman on that night, and I ripped him one. And so evidently the tone was too harsh against, basically people inside the club. Let's just keep it real.

"So, the message was very clear, and I walked out of that meeting thinking, 'No, I'm definitely not going to do that.' So, if they take me off the air, they take me off the air. But there's no way in the world I'm going to kowtow to these guys saying, 'Take it easy on anybody inside of Washington.' It's the antithesis of what I do."

Cenk had a decision to make. Very similar to the one Bret Baier had to make, and what everyone else working at mainstream media outlets is faced with at one point or another. "Do I play ball and do what my bosses are wanting me to do, or do I stay true to who I am as a journalist and report honest, hard-hitting news?"

Unlike Baier, Cenk chose the latter, and that's why we don't see him in the mainstream media anymore. He's actually resented by the mainstream media, the Democratic establishment, and the financial elites of this country because of this. There are some other reasons as well, but we will get to those later.

Uygur left that meeting more determined than ever to continue doing what he believed was right and what he thought journalism should be about. He continued to hit both Democrat and Republican politicians hard, not discriminating between who he held accountable. Sure enough, this is exactly what the people wanted. His ratings went up because he was honest.

"I didn't play ball," Uygur said. "What I did do was I then went on air and started, if anything, hitting the Democrats, Obama, Washington, harder.

"So what wound up happening is I ended up getting great ratings. There was this fascinating phenomenon where, if I criticized Obama, my ratings in that fifteen-minute block would go down and you could see clear as day, because it makes people uncomfortable. It's their beloved Obama, they're watching MSNBC. You know they want you to tell them good fairy tales and that he's a saint. But the next day they would rise and that happened over and over and over again. So, what they realized is that 'This guy is different. I'm not sure what he's going to say, as opposed to other MSNBC hosts, which you're absolutely positive what they're going to say. There's no question of what they're going to say. And maybe I could trust him, because you know he seems to be his own man and he's being honest about criticizing even the people he likes.'"

Do you think MSNBC was happy with Uygur's blatant disregard for his directives? If you do, you'd be wrong. They weren't happy and Uygur got called back into the executive's office.

"So then in June, Phil Griffin calls me back in and says, 'Cenk, I'm going to move you to the weekends, so you're not getting the six o'clock spot,'" Uygur said.

Uygur was being demoted because he didn't follow directions and although he thought he knew how the mainstream media worked at the time, he was still caught off guard.

"The funny thing is, I'm still surprised. After all that, all I had talked about, this phenomenon and I knew the phenomenon, and then it happened to me," Uygur said. "But still, I was surprised because my ratings were so good. I thought, 'That will protect me, right?'"

When he was being told he was being moved down, Uygur decided to question it and try to find out what it was he did wrong.

"So, I asked Phil this one question that I think was determinative," Uygur said. "I said, 'Phil, are my ratings good?'

"He said, 'Yea, of course.'

"I said, 'Do I cause any trouble internally? Is that an issue or anything?'

"He's like, 'No, no, you're a great team player, everyone likes you.'

"So then I said, 'If you move me to the weekends, under what circumstance could I possibly move back into prime time, if it's not the ratings and it's not any of these other factors?'

"He was just stumped," Uygur continued. "He didn't think I was going to ask him that question. He had not thought about it. He can't say the real reason, so it was the most awkward minute of silence that anyone has ever lived through. So, he literally didn't have an answer, and then we just moved on.

"So that told me, 'Of course, I told you not to shit on the establishment and you did. So that's why you're getting moved down and you're not going to get moved back up. And maybe the only way you get moved back up is if you start learning how to kiss ass.'

"So that was my perception of what he was saying."

This is a pretty telling exchange. It illustrates the problem with our mainstream news media more than just about anything out there could. If an anchor is getting good ratings and isn't causing internal issues, there is no reason they should be demoted. However, Cenk was demoted, and the fact Griffin couldn't give him an answer as to why is just sad. If you're the president of the network and your main objective isn't to report the honest truth, as wrong as that is, you should at least have the decency to tell your employee the truth of why they are being demoted.

To make matters worse, MSNBC actually offered to pay more money for Uygur's reduced role. They wanted to shut him up, but Uygur wasn't going to have it.

"They offered to double my salary and it was for me, I mean you have to remember, before MSNBC, my entire career, I'd never made above fifty thousand dollars," Uygur said. "I think I averaged like seventeen thousand dollars a year. And so, when they offered to double my salary, to move me to one day a week, which is like the easiest job in the world, and it's a three-year contract, ooouff."

"So luckily, I'm married to a saint and she was like, 'Nahh, it's okay.' She was like, 'Look, I married you when you were poor, and you're still poor, that's fine, nothing's changed, we never got used to the money, so it's okay.' And so, I turned it down and they were pretty flabbergasted.

"I left, and then I did a big talk on *Young Turks* about why I left, and I was a persona non grata from that moment forward, not just at MSNBC, but really anywhere in DC," Uygur said.

So, Uygur said no. He stayed true to who he was and refused to be censored by the system. He said he made the decision based on a matter of principle, and everyone there at the time thought he was an idiot for doing so.

What would you do if you were in that exact situation? You have an offer on the table to have your salary doubled to work just one day a week? You'd probably take it, right? Like the people at MSNBC said, you'd have to be an idiot to turn that down, right?

I know if I were a journalist working at one of these mainstream establishment outlets and I had a family I was looking out for, it would be really hard to turn that offer down, no matter how principled I was. It's just human nature in our current society.

Uygur said most journalists wouldn't be able to turn that offer down because these outlets have such a tight grip on these journalists. He said the only reason he was able to be the tough guy and act on principle by turning the offer down was he had a huge audience to fall back on. He had TYT, which he always viewed as his real career anyway, to act as a safety net for him, but most other hosts, reporters, or journalists don't have something like that.

"But for the other hosts, if you stop working at MSNBC, where are you going to go?" Uygur said. "You can't go to Fox News. You likely can't go to CNN. There's literally nowhere else to go, so they got you. After MSNBC is the abyss.

"So that's what happened to Ed Schultz. He kind of drew the line at some point, I don't know that inside story, but he went back to radio for a little while and realized there is no radio, radio's dead. And then he went to RT (Russian TV America) because there is nowhere to go! So, they've got these hosts by the balls."

That they do, Cenk, that they do.

Uygur mentioned Ed Schultz as an example of someone who had nowhere to go after MSNBC. He said he didn't really know what happened to him, but lucky for us, Schultz told his story before he sadly passed away in 2018.[161]

Ed Schultz was the host of *The Ed Show*, a weekday news program on MSNBC. The show aired from 2009 to 2015. Starting in 2004 and continuing throughout his time at MSNBC,

---

161 Richard Sandomir, "Ed Schultz, Blunt-Spoken Political Talk-Show Host, Dies at 64," *The New York Times*, July 5, 2018.

Schultz also hosted *The Ed Schultz Show*, a talk-radio show. He transitioned his show to a podcast titled *Ed Schultz News and Commentary* in 2015, which he operated until his death in 2018. After Schultz's dismissal from MSNBC in 2015, he went on to host *News with Ed Schultz* on RT America.[162] He held this position until the day he died.

Schultz was interviewed on *The Jamie Weinstein Show* in 2018, where he talked about his time at MSNBC and why he was ultimately dismissed.[163] Schultz believed he was let go at MSNBC because he was sympathetic to Bernie Sanders. He described the events that made him think this, and it's a story that is another exhibit of how the mainstream media in this country is not made up of independent, objective, journalistic institutions.

Schultz started off by describing his relationship with Sanders.

"Well, Bernie Sanders is a very good friend of mine," Schultz said. "And even though I'm at RT now and a lot of relations have been severed, and we're, so to speak, disconnected because I'm anchoring the news on RT America, Bernie is still a very good friend of mine. I did support him; my wife contributed monthly to his campaign." [164]

---

162 Matthew Sheffield, "Krystal Ball: MSNBC Never Wanted Ed Schultz's Working Class Audience," *The Hill*, July 6, 2018.

163 David Rutz, "Ed Schultz Suggests MSNBC Fired Him Because of Bernie Sanders Support," April 16, 2018, video, 8:59.

164 Ibid.

He went on to describe how he would have Sanders on his shows and the potential he saw in him.

"I guess when I got to MSNBC in 2009, I brought Bernie Sanders to cable probably more than anybody else," Schultz said. "He was a senator, rather obscure, from the small state of Vermont and, of course, I was new to the cable world. And so, I had had Bernie on my radio show numerous times, and so I put him on TV. The more we put him on, the more I told my teams, 'You gotta listen to this guy.' I mean, this is where our listeners are on *the Ed Schultz* radio show, this guy is speaking to the millennials. He is speaking to the younger generation. He is speaking about a future. He is somewhat Kennedyish, so to speak. He had a vision for the country, he talked about change, and I thought that he was going to go, and he did. And I thought he was going to take off politically, and eventually, it took him years, but he did. So, Bernie is a good friend, and I believe in what he stands for." [165]

Before discussing a story that made it clear the network was not fond of Sanders, Schultz described the differences between the day-to-day operations at MSNBC and at RT America.

"I want to make this very clear, and I hope your audience consumes this," Schultz said. "There was more oversight and more direction given to me on content at MSNBC than there ever has been here at RT. And I think that it's very sad that story is not getting out. Many times I was told what to lead with on MSNBC, many times I was told what I was not going

---

165 Ibid.

to do, and I've got a story that, had I not been involved in it, I would have never believed it. Phil Griffin, who I consider a friend to this day, was a watchdog, far more than anything I am exposed to here at RT America." [166]

This sentiment expressed by Schultz seems pretty familiar to the stories Uygur told me about MSNBC and Phil Griffin. The story he is referring to has to do with MSNBC's coverage of Sanders in the 2016 Democratic primary and foreshadows why Schultz believes he was ultimately let go at MSNBC. Later in the interview with Weinstein, Schultz told this very story.

"In fact, when Bernie Sanders was announcing that he was going to be a candidate for the nomination of the Democratic party in Burlington, Vermont, I was the only cable host between Fox, MSNBC, and CNN that was there live to cover it," Schultz said. "Now there were live cameras there, but we had coordinated with the Sanders campaign that at five o'clock he was going to make his announcement, and we were going to cover this on *The Ed Show*." [167]

This sounds like a pretty big scoop for *The Ed Show* and MSNBC. A sitting US senator announcing he's running for president, and you're the only network there to cover it live. It's quite the exclusive, if you'd ask me. In the age of everyone in journalism wanting to be first, or to have an exclusive interview, one would think MSNBC would be thrilled about Schultz's reporting.

---

166 Ibid.
167 Ibid.

"I go to Bernie Sanders's house that afternoon, for an interview in the backyard, about a fifteen-minute interview," Schultz continued. "The grandkids are running around, it's a big day for the Sanders family. He's going to announce that he's running for president. We're going to carry it live later on in the day, and we're going to run this one-on-one take with Bernie." [168]

Like I said, it seems like a pretty big scene any objective media outlet would want to be covering, but apparently, that wasn't the case.

"Three thousand people are there on Lake Champagne, it's five minutes to air, and I get a phone call from Phil Griffin," Schultz said. "'You're not covering this!' [169]

"I said, 'Phil, Bernie Sanders is announcing he's running for president. He's going to be president.'

"'I don't care! You're not covering this.' And it got rather contentious." [170]

Schultz's story was interrupted with the phrase, "Why though?" Schultz brushed it off and quickly continued on.

"Now you're asking me for opinion, but I'm giving you fact right now about what happened, and other people, who were

168 Ibid.
169 Ibid.
170 Ibid.

there with me, will attest the fact and back me up that this is what happened," Schultz said. [171]

"We were told that we had to cover something down in Texas that was totally meaningless and another press conference in Baltimore, which had already been in the news for a few days. [172]

"We had Bernie Sanders live. We were coordinating with his campaign, and I'm told five minutes before, 'You're not covering Bernie Sanders.'" [173]

Obviously, there was a disdain for Bernie Sanders that was present in the mainstream media, and it turns out, Schultz's desire to give Sanders's his fair shot on-air may have been what ultimately did him in.

"I think the Clintons were connected to Andy Lack, connected at the hip," Schultz said. "I think that they didn't want anybody in their prime time or anywhere in their lineup supporting Bernie Sanders. I think that they were in the tank for Hillary Clinton and I think it was managed, and forty-five days later, I was out at MSNBC. And I thought it stunk, they gave me my contract, I signed a non-disclosure agreement and also no bad-mouthing agreement, which I felt good with because I thought that this was overtime all going to wash out. And I knew if Bernie Sanders didn't win,

---

171 Ibid.

172 Ibid.

173 Ibid.

he was going to run again because the man is determined, so I was patient, took my money, and went on." [174]

It's a pretty strong claim by Schultz, but when you consider everything that went on in the election cycles of 2016 and 2020 with Bernie Sanders and the mainstream media, it's very believable.

The point is had Ed Schultz done what his bosses wanted him to do with a smile on his face—agreed to shun Sanders and keep his anti-corporate views off the air—Schultz may never have lost his job at MSNBC.

It also supports Cenk Uygur's claim when someone loses their spot in the mainstream media, there really isn't anywhere for them to go. Ed Schultz went from being on one of the most popular cable networks in America to being on RT America. So, this fear of not having a reliable job anywhere else is a big obstacle averting journalists from choosing to stay objective and go against their corporate executives' desires by reporting complete, wholesome, and truthful information. It's easier, and sometimes necessary, to just do what their executives say.

Another obstacle preventing journalists in the mainstream media from being the objective truth-seekers they're supposed to be is simply working in the mainstream media is pretty awesome. There are a lot of perks and Uygur detailed them in his conversation with me.

---

174 Ibid.

"The other thing you have to realize, Owen, is that when you are a host on a cable news channel like MSNBC, the world's your oyster," Uygur told me. "It's amazing how well people treat you. Oh my god, you are feted."

He went on to describe the many perks he experienced when he was a host at MSNBC, before he opted to turn down the luxurious offer to be demoted.

"I mean, the Turkish American Society, which didn't know me at all before then, or barely knew me, it didn't matter how many billions of views I've gotten online, all of a sudden, I'm the champion of the world, and I must have gotten three Turkish American awards in one year at that point," Uygur said.

"I'm getting speech requests and people just treat you differently. I mean, you become like a lord in this royalty. So, I'm flying first-class, and I've never flown first-class before in my life.

"So, it was just amazing, and I was told by the Young Turks audience, 'I didn't know they had warm nuts in first-class.' I know it sounds funny, that's the point. But, like, they gratuitously warm up the nuts that they serve you in first-class."

Uygur continued on to explain even more perks. This next story is my personal favorite; I think you will enjoy it as well.

"I remember one time at MSNBC, I had to go back to New Jersey, but it was Labor Day, so it was going to be crazy crowded," Uygur said. "So long story short on that, I just didn't know how to take my giant bag back to New Jersey from New York. And they actually paid to have someone drive my bag, independently of me, to my parent's house in New Jersey."

Yeah, that's pretty sweet, I could see where it would be hard to give that up. The nicest perk I've ever had was free golf after-hours at a golf course I worked at in high school, and it got dark, so it wasn't that great. It's safe to say having a private ride for my luggage, provided on the company's dime, would be a step up for me, and I'm assuming a lot of people out there.

Uygur mentioned one of Chris Rock's jokes when describing his luxurious lifestyle when he worked at MSNBC.

"Chris Rock has this joke about how if poor people knew how good rich people had it, there already would've been a revolution," Uygur said while laughing.

Yep, rich people in America have it very well, and from the sounds of it, the hosts and journalists in the mainstream media happen to be among them.

A lifestyle like this can be very hard to turn down. It also can give people a pretty big ego.

Ironically, early on in Uygur's tenure at MSNBC, he got a warning about this very concern to look out for from someone who now may have one of the biggest egos on cable news. Yes, none other than Rachel Maddow herself, told Uygur to be careful about getting too high a sense of himself.

"Rachel Maddow, right before I started, was really nice to me, and we know each other from Air American," Uygur said. "You know, we were acquaintances, it is fair to say, to some degree friends, and she took me to breakfast and said, 'The one thing that you really have to watch out for is television warps you, and if you're not careful, it'll get to your head and cause damage. Good people go in and then they get surrounded by yes-men and then start to get a view of themselves as high and mighty.'

"I loved that speech. I thought she was so right, and I was totally cognizant of that. I might want to give that same speech back to her at this point, but that's another story."

So, these are the obstacles facing journalists from being objective, fair, and only reporting true information. The structure incentivizes swimming in the direction the corporate owners want and keeping to their agendas more than practicing good, honest journalism. It promotes those who do what the executives want, like Bret Baier, and filters out those who choose to diverge from the executive directives to be objective, like what happened to Cenk Uygur and Ed Schultz.

The journalists who carve out prominent careers at the mainstream outlets have done so by making the choice to follow directions rather than being objective. This isn't a good thing for the quality of news in America; in fact, it's a very bad thing. However, it's not right to fault the individual hosts and journalists themselves. As we've seen in this chapter, there's typically nowhere else for them to go if they choose to be good, honest journalists, and, well, life is pretty good for them, so why would they throw that away? I know a lot of other people wouldn't.

What can be blamed and what we can change is this system of corporate ownership. There shouldn't be corporate agendas that are present in the mainstream media. Our media should be free to report the truth and only the truth, no matter what it is, just like our Founding Fathers intended. We as Americans deserve this, and we can have it.

CHAPTER 7

GROUPTHINK IN THE NEWSROOM

There is a clear system of filtration that takes place in the American mainstream media. If you're at odds with the corporate interests that own the media, you won't have a place there for long, if you're even hired in the first place.

This system was summed up very precisely by Noam Chomsky, author of the book *Manufacturing Consent*, as well as many others.

Chomsky was being interviewed by a BBC host when the topic of censorship in the media came up. The host asked Chomsky how he could know if he, the host, was self-censoring. Chomsky's response was short and hit the nail on the head.

"I don't say you're self-censoring," Chomsky responded. "I'm sure you believe everything that you're saying, but what I am saying is, if you believed something different, you wouldn't be sitting where you are sitting." [175]

Chomsky is exactly right. It is by no accident people like Cenk Uygur don't last in the prime-time slots the mainstream news media of the United States has to offer. In this same interview, Chomsky detailed how this system of filtration goes beyond the news media and starts well before we venture off into our professional careers. He referenced George Orwell's proposed preface to *Animal Farm*.

"Orwell, you may recall, has an essay about literary censorship in England, which was supposed to be the introduction to *Animal Farm*, except that it never appeared," Chomsky states. "He points out, 'Look, I'm writing about a totalitarian society, but in free, democratic England, it's not all that different,' and then he says, 'Unpopular ideas can be silenced without any force.'" [176]

Chomsky continues citing Orwell. "He gives a two-sentence response which isn't very profound, but captures it. He says, 'Two reasons: first, the press is owned by wealthy men who have every interest in not having certain things appear, but second, the whole educational system, from beginning on through, just gets you to understand that there are certain

---

175   Glenn Greenwald (@ggreenwald), "Many journalists - either for self-serv-
        ing reasons or due to genuine befuddlement - are completely misinter-
        preting Bernie's media critique.," Twitter video, August 13, 2019.
176   Ibid.

things you just don't say.' Well, spelling these things out, that's perfectly correct." [177]

After being interrupted with a question about journalists' self-censoring, Chomsky gets into the details about the system of filtration that takes place from a young age.

"No, not self-censoring," Chomsky states. "There's a filtering system that starts in kindergarten and goes all the way through, and it's not going to work 100 percent, but it's pretty effective. It selects for obedience and subordination." [178]

The host interjected by saying someone who is hard to deal with wouldn't make it.

Chomsky agreed and said, "Behavior problems, if you read applications to a graduate school, you'll see that people will tell you he's not, he doesn't get along too well with his colleagues, you know how to interpret those things." [179]

Chomsky and Orwell's indictment of the UK's filtration system rings uncomfortably true across the pond as well, where we see the same problems in the US media. This system of filtration that is in effect in the mainstream media in the United States starts off well before journalists are applying for jobs.

---

177 Ibid.
178 Ibid.
179 Ibid.

People are taught to follow directions and do what is required to get a good grade, not necessarily what is right. In school, we aren't even always doing what is best for our learning. Think about it. How many times did you have a test coming up, and instead of learning the material, you just memorized it because that was the best way to get the grade? If you're anything like me, you probably did that quite a bit. We needed that good grade on the test more than we needed to learn the subject matter. We needed the grade in order to get a good grade in class, in order to have a high GPA, in order to be accepted into college. Then we had to do this all over again in order to graduate college. We had to graduate college because it was the only way to get a good job. If we failed at any of this, our lives would be a miserable failure.

Of course, that isn't true; just ask anyone who didn't go to college, you can live a decent life without going to college, just as you can have a miserable life with going to college. But nonetheless, it's what kids are told. So, when someone graduates college, they have spent seventeen years of their lives doing what they are told, doing whatever is necessary to please their teachers, to get the good grade, and ultimately graduate college. We were trained to do not what we thought was best for us or other people, but whatever was the easiest way to get to the next level, or as Chomsky would say, we were trained to be obedient.

Now, this may seem unrelated to news in America, but it isn't. This is the beginning of the filter.

If you want to be a journalist at a mainstream outlet in the United States, you will notice one very basic requirement everywhere you apply: you need a college degree. This simple requirement filters out anyone who didn't have the necessary levels of obedience to make it through school. This means from the beginning, the vast majority of our journalists were trained to be obedient to positions of authority, not to challenge them.

As we know, the mainstream media outlets deliberately select people who are more in line with the networks' corporates interests for these positions. This virtually assures the outcome of newsrooms across the country being made up of people with very similar ideas and experiences.

However, as Chomsky mentioned, not all filters are perfect. Just like when someone is cleaning a pool with a net and they get the leaves and other big objects out, but the smaller, less obvious debris isn't cleaned out of the pool, the system of filtration in place at mainstream media outlets filters out a lot of unwanted debris, like journalists who make it their duty to challenge the status quo and pursue truth no matter where it takes them. However, some smaller, less obvious particles still get through.

So, what does this mean? Well, it means even after the Cenk Uygurs of the world are filtered out of the mainstream media outlets across this country, there are still some journalists in these newsrooms who are there for the right reasons. They have a desire to report the objective truth.

These reporters are unwanted, but they got through the initial stage of filtration. They are different from most of the journalists in the newsroom, based on their perspectives and beliefs; however, they are overwhelmingly similar in one big way. They all have a college degree, and because of this, they have had obedience to positions of authority drilled into their souls. This allows for the concept of groupthink to come into play and ensure ideas that may be contrary to what the corporate owners of the media want out there are never actually published or aired.

Groupthink is a term that refers to the psychological phenomenon where people will strive for consensus within a group. People will set aside their own personal beliefs or adopt the opinion of the rest of the group just to maintain peace and harmony.[180] This term was first used by social psychologist Irving L. Janis in 1972.[181] Those who participate in groupthink are people who are opposed to the decisions or opinion of the group as a whole, but frequently remain quiet because they prefer to keep the peace rather than disrupt the cohesiveness and uniformity of the group.[182]

This psychological phenomenon happens all the time in newsrooms across the country, and it helps filter out perspectives and stories that are unfavorable to the corporate interests that own the news. The reason for this is pretty straightforward. Due to the system's selecting of journalists who have similar viewpoints as their corporate overlords, the majority opinion and/or perspective is in line with what

---

180 Kendra Cherry, "What Is Groupthink?," *verywellmind*, updated November 12, 2020.

181 Ibid.

182 Ibid.

the corporate owners believe or want to be published in the news virtually all of the time.

Since the system is not perfect, and some journalists are still willing to report the objective truth, there are sometimes stories pitched that are at odds with the corporate-friendly agendas at the mainstream outlets. Rather than being aired or made public, these are typically always crushed by groupthink. The reporters who found the story will bring it up to their editors or executive producers in meetings; there may be fellow reporters and journalists present as well. The majority of the group will scoff at it, not be willing to really give it the light of day, or change the story entirely, and rather than fighting on behalf of the story, the original journalist who reported on it will instead go with the group's ideas because it's easier. They don't want to cause any problems.

This pressure to conform is real and has been drilled into journalists since they were young.

I've had direct experience with groupthink in the newsroom. I've actually been a part of it, and not fought for the best, most accurate version of a story, because I didn't want to cause any conflict with my editor or my more senior co-workers.

I worked as a sports reporter for the *Minnesota Daily*, the campus newspaper at the University of Minnesota. I was covering the University of Minnesota men's hockey team for a weekend series and in my series recap, I wanted to focus on puck possession and how the University of Minnesota Golden Gophers were out-possessed the entire weekend, and how their lack of ability to sustain time in the offensive zone would be problematic going forward, even though they managed to win one of the games that weekend.

My editor was someone who'd never played hockey and didn't know the sport that well. He didn't want me to do the story that way, because the shots on goal were close to even and the Gophers split the series; they won one game and the opposing team won once. He wanted me to write the story as if the series was played fairly even, but it wasn't. The Gophers were thoroughly outplayed. They were pinned in their zone for the majority of the series and the shot attempts reflected that. I wanted to use that statistic in my story, as that is one of the best statistics for measuring puck possession in hockey. The reason this is better than shots on goal is it counts all shot attempts, no matter if they end up on the net, are blocked, or go wide.

A team can be in the offensive zone for minutes on end and have numerous shot attempts, but may not actually get a shot on the net. The shot attempts statistic takes this into account and is why it is a better measurement for possession. It's possible for a team to out-attempt a team by a large margin, but end up being outshot because their shots weren't getting through to the net. This is exactly what happened in this series. The Gophers were out-attempted by a severe margin but ended up close to even in shots on goal.

Now if you're confused by those statistical measurements in hockey, that's okay. This book is about the news media, not hockey. The point is the version of the story I originally wanted to write would have been the most accurate portrayal of what had happened, yet it wasn't published because I gave in to groupthink.

I knew better than my editor. I was more experienced with hockey; I'd played and watched it my whole life and he hadn't. My version was a better representation of the series, but he wanted me to change it because he didn't understand the statistics I was referring to. Rather than fighting him on it and trying to push my original version of the story through, I changed it and went with what my editor was suggesting. I did it because I thought it was the easiest thing to do. I thought it would avoid conflict with my editor, which I figured was a necessity for me to move up at the paper. I had allowed a less accurate story to be published, solely to maintain a more peaceful relationship with my direct superior, my editor.

This was groupthink at work in the newsroom, groupthink leading to non-objective reporting. Now sure, you may say, "Who cares, it's just an article from some college paper about some dumb hockey game," and you'd be right. That story didn't really matter. Who cares if I called out the Gophers' lack of O-zone time or not? The fans maybe do, but it's not life or death. It's not about their healthcare, war, or what the president plans to do in a global pandemic. This is all true, but the fact is there is a pressure to conform to the beliefs of your superiors journalists have to face, and typically, that pressure wins and the journalists conform to the preferred perspective.

If an example from a college newspaper isn't enough for you to understand the dynamics of groupthink, here is groupthink on display in another newsroom, this time at MSNBC.

In my interview with David Shuster, he described one such instance.

"When I was at MSNBC, and I was covering the [Lewis] Scooter Libby trial, and you know the way the evidence came in, it was pretty clear to us, that by putting all the evidence in the case, that Vice President Chaney was ordering his chief of staff Scooter Libby to dig up dirt on Valerie Plame and her husband Joe Wilson, who had written a *New York Times* op-ed critical of Cheney," Shuster told me. "Well, nobody else had gone there yet, to the vice president, to say that it was clear that the vice president was ordering Scooter Libby. Well, I went with that report, and I got hammered for it. Until a few weeks later, when in the trial they played the Scooter Libby deposition and sure enough, Dick Chaney's giving him orders."

Shuster's report was right, but no one in the mainstream media believed him because it went against their way of thinking. Scenarios like this happen all the time, and far too often, the reporter ends up not going with the story because they don't want to ruffle the feathers and disturb the harmony at their workplace; the psychological term for this: groupthink. Fortunately, Shuster is one of the good guys and went with his report, and luckily, he only had to deal with a few weeks of being hassled because the trial happened to prove him right.

"In the mainstream media, I think [groupthink] plays a huge role," Shuster said. "There's a very strong groupthink in how you cover stories and what the stories are.

"I think there's a natural reluctance if you're in the mainstream media to take risks, because if you take risks, if you go out on a limb, it could be more damaging to your career. You're seen as something of a loose cannon. Unless it's a really compelling sort of scoop, if it's sort of a questionable scoop, but even if you think it's solid, there's just not an incentive now in the mainstream media to go out on a limb. As a result, there is this sort of perverse incentive of 'well, the *New York Times* is reporting it this way, the *Washington Post* is reporting it this way, or CBS News or NBC is reporting it this way, so that's the way we should be reporting it.'"

Shuster's getting at the same thing I was. He's saying journalists don't want to push for stories that may be viewed as "out-there" or "unpopular" because it could hurt their careers. He's definitely correct here. And what are the stories that would be viewed at as "out-there" or "unpopular," you ask? Well, they aren't necessarily the stories that would be unpopular to the general public. They're the stories that are viewed as "out-there" and "unpopular" by the journalists at the mainstream outlets and their corporate owners. This isn't a very diverse group of people; they all are highly paid, have high-quality health insurance, are college-educated, and live in big coastal cities. They don't have the same life experiences as everyday Americans; therefore, they don't view stories in the same light the general public does.

Concepts such as Medicare-for-all are portrayed in a very negative light in the mainstream media because the people who work there can't fathom the necessity of such a proposal. They don't understand what it's like to not have quality healthcare. They think it would just be an unnecessary government expense that wouldn't have any real effect on their lives. All of the people they work with have similar thoughts, and for that reason, if someone ever proposes to do a piece on the benefits of a Medicare-for-all, single-payer healthcare system in the United States, it's met with eye-rolls or contempt, because the people who work in the mainstream media are living in a bubble, isolated from the rest of the country.

They don't think the public wants Medicare-for-all, when in fact, they overwhelmingly do. In an April 19–20, 2020, poll of registered voters, 69 percent of Americans supported a Medicare-for-all, single-payer system.[183] That's nearly 70 percent of Americans, yet the policy proposal is still covered negatively in the mainstream media. There's no reason for this to be an unpopular topic, yet it is treated that way. This is a perfect display of the effects groupthink has on the news coming from mainstream media outlets.

Steve Bannon, the former executive chair of Breitbart News and a former White House chief strategist under former president Trump, once summed up the groupthink dynamic in the news media better than anyone ever could.

---

183 Gabriela Schulte, "Poll: 69 Percent of Voters Support Medicare for All," *The Hill*, April 24, 2020.

"The media bubble is the ultimate symbol of what's wrong with this country," Bannon said. "It's just a circle of people talking to themselves who have no fucking idea what's going on." [184]

Now Bannon certainly isn't the brightest guy on the planet either, but his depiction of what is going on in the media is spot-on. The people at these outlets socialize with one another and are friends. In their day-to-day lives, they interact with each other, not the average American living in Michigan, Minnesota, Nebraska, or anywhere other than their coastal bubbles. They don't understand the problems real Americans are dealing with, and this ensures any populist idea or viewpoint that comes from average Americans and is pitched to the media is viewed as an unpopular idea, and there is no reason to report on it or cover it fairly.

The Occupy Wallstreet movement was a perfect case study on the biases of the mainstream media that result from groupthink. This was a movement that resonated with many, many people and was a precursor for the populist presidential campaigns we saw in 2016, both Trump and Sanders, yet there was virtually no coverage of this in the mainstream media.

Shuster told me the newsrooms he worked in were fairly diverse, in the sense they had African-Americans and women, but his sense was there were certain stories that still just never broke through. He thought the Occupy movement was one of the best examples.

---

184 Jack Shafer and Tucker Doherty, "The Media Bubble Is Worse Than You Think," *PoliticoMagazine*, May/June 2017.

"I thought [the Occupy movement] was a big story," Shuster said. "I thought it sort of showed that this was the populism that is beginning to sort of push back against corporate interests and Wall Street interests. You could not [find] a network newscast with that story. There was very limited coverage in the *New York Times*, *Washington Post*, the main newspapers. I was at Current TV at the time, and we decided to go against the grain. Keith Olbermann was really into it, and so we did a lot of stories on Occupy Wallstreet, but people looked at us, in the rest of the media, like we had three heads. It was like, 'Ugh, you guys are in bed with those silly socialists or whatever.'

"Well, the thing is that the Occupy Democrats, the Occupy Wall Street, that sort of became the precursor for the populism that we saw in 2016, with Bernie Sanders on the left, and Donald Trump on the right. There were a lot of people in this country who agreed with the Occupy Wallstreet folks, that the wealth gap is getting bigger and growing too fast and there's not enough taxes on the wealthy and not enough help for the working class. This was sort of a precursor to all of that, that most of the media missed."

Shuster's right again. The Occupy movement was a precursor to everything we've seen since 2016, yet the mainstream media missed it entirely. They missed it for two main reasons: it goes against their corporate owners' interests, which are the same as Wall Street's; and as Bannon put it, they don't know what the fuck is going on. The groupthink is too much. Most of them are doing great financially and don't interact with the people of this country who are really hurting.

Therefore, they couldn't comprehend why people would be upset at the status quo.

Cenk Uygur discussed this groupthink phenomenon with me as well. He talked about how it leads to good independent reporters being viewed as problematic because they aren't sticking to the establishment point of view, or the perspective that is most prevalent at these outlets.

"My overall thought is, they're all [mainstream media outlets, and journalists at these institutions] protectors of the realm and not in a good way, the corrupt realm and they largely don't know it," Uygur said. "So, for cable news, it's so obvious because you are on the air, so the minute you stray from the establishment way of thinking, you're going to get reminders. I've never worked in a newsroom before, so I don't know how that system works, but my guess is that your editors just edit it out and certain people get promotions and certain people don't.

"You begin to realize, don't do what Glen Greenwald does, do not do what David Sirota does. And the groupthink is so thick that as David Sirota breaks one amazing story after another, they all genuinely convince themselves that 'Ahh, no, he's just a rabble-rouser, he's a gadfly.' Gadfly, wait, isn't that what all journalists are supposed to be? Aren't they supposed to, I forget the exact quote, but afflict the powerful and comfort the powerless? Instead, what they wind up doing is comforting the powerful and afflicting the powerless. So 'Medicare-for-all, we're never going to give you that, you think we're going to give you healthcare? Hell no. You think we're going to save the planet? No, you losers, we can't afford that. Oh, tax breaks, for the rich? Well obviously, that's very sensible.'"

Uygur is saying journalists at the mainstream media stick to the way of thinking their corporate overlords want them to and because the vast majority of them do it, anyone who dares to think any differently is ostracized and demonized. This leads to a direct lack of objectivity and wholesome reporting at our mainstream media outlets.

The mainstream media selects people who have political beliefs and ideologies that are similar to those of their corporate owners and the political establishment of this country. In addition to this, the vast majority of these journalists are highly paid and working in the coastal regions, typically in the big cities like New York, Washington, DC, and Los Angeles. [185]

This causes there to be a severe lack of diversity of thought and lived experiences in the mainstream media. Now some journalists possess different beliefs and manage to find their way into a job at a mainstream media outlet, but they either stay silent and go along with the party line due to groupthink, or they try to be the idealistic journalists they desired to be and report the news no matter what it is. If they choose the former, they keep their jobs and all is harmonious; if they choose the latter, they are demonized by the rest of the mainstream media and are eventually out of a job.

---

185 Ibid.

The majority of these journalists who possess beliefs contrary to those of their corporate owners choose to stay silent and swim in the direction their superiors want. They make this choice for a multitude of reasons: one, they have had obedience to authority and positions of power drilled into them through their entire journey through the educational system in this country; and two, they're afraid to go against the majority opinion of their respective journalistic outlets because they don't want to cause conflict with their superiors and thereby put their jobs, careers, and cozy lifestyles at risk.

This whole system that is in place at the mainstream media outlets, the selection process, the filtration system, the groupthink, all of it leads to a press that is dangerously lacking in objectivity and understanding of issues that affect everyday Americans. This lack of objectivity is by design, it is no accident, and it has extreme effects on the politics and economics of our country.

CHAPTER 8

MAINSTREAM MEDIA'S POLITICAL EFFECTS

———

There are considerably more profitable industries than the news business, so why would billionaires, who could buy into anything, want to own the media?

The answer is because owning the mainstream media helps them craft and preserve a political landscape that is beneficial to them, and not the American people as a whole.

The mainstream media in the United States has the power to affect elections and formulate the public debate in our country. This is not a good thing, because this ability leads to our government serving the financial elite of our country and not the country as a whole.

America has 320 million people living in it. That is a lot of people, and there is no way one individual person could speak to each and every person in this country. Therefore, candidates for public office must rely on other forms of communication to get their message out to the masses. They can buy ads on TV, they can buy ads in newspapers, they can buy ads on the radio, they can buy ads online, they can hold rallies, and they can appear on podcasts. All of these are good ways to reach people, but airtime isn't cheap. Candidates can't solely rely on paid media to get their message out, because they simply don't have enough money, unless they're Mike Bloomberg.

So where do they turn? The mainstream media. Yes, candidates rely on our country's news media to help them get their message out. They call this free media, or media coverage that appears as news and not paid advertisements.[186] Since candidates are relying on the media to help relay their campaign's messaging to Americans, it affords the media outlets a great amount of power to dictate how these elections turn out. They are able to select who they cover fairly and who they don't cover fairly. If the media doesn't give all the candidates equal amounts of coverage, and they aren't fair with their reporting, it puts some candidates at great advantages while putting others at significant disadvantages. This is an immense responsibility the media possesses.

In a country where the press was free, fair, and objective, this wouldn't be an issue. However, this is the United States, and as we know, a free and objective press is something we don't have. The mainstream media is owned by billionaires and billion-dollar corporations, so they make sure to take advantage of this responsibility that is presented to them.

---

186 The Texas Politics Project, "Free Media versus Earned Media," *University of Texas at Austin*, accessed January 26, 2021.

Rather than doing what the Founding Fathers intended and providing hard-hitting objective reporting to keep the powerful in check, the mainstream media does all they can to ensure corporate-friendly politicians are elected and remain in office, while candidates at odds with corporate interests are squashed.

No matter what you think of him or his politics, there is no better example of this phenomenon than Bernie Sanders and the mainstream media's coverage of him in his last two campaigns for the presidency in 2016 and 2020, respectively.

The independent senator from Vermont has always been a strong supporter of the working class. He's one of the very few politicians in the history of our country to stay consistent in his beliefs and values throughout his long political career. First, as mayor of Burlington, Vermont, from 1981 to 89, then as a member of the US House of Representatives from 1991 to 2007, and now as a US senator from Vermont, a position he has held since 2007. Sanders has not been shy about calling out corporate America and how the politics of our country have been rigged to benefit the financial elites of this country at the expense of everyone else.

He calls out how the wealthy don't pay their fair share of taxes, how the bankers on Wall Street destroyed our economy and got away with it in 2008, and how the health insurance and drug companies are preying on everyday Americans. With Sanders's critiques of corporate America in mind, it comes as no surprise Sanders is disliked by the billionaire class in America.

Sanders has never been the beneficiary of positive coverage in the media. However, his presidential campaigns, both in 2016 and 2020, saw the distaste for him by the mainstream media taken to new heights.

A perfect example of this is Ed Schultz's story we covered in Chapter 6. Do you remember it? Schultz was going to cover Sanders's 2015 rally on Lake Champlain in Burlington, Vermont, where Sanders was going to announce he was running for president. There were thousands of people there; it was a big deal, but Schultz got a call from an angry Phil Griffin just five minutes before he was supposed to go on air demanding he didn't cover Sanders.[187] This contempt for Sanders by the mainstream media was not an isolated incident. It was on display over and over again in 2016 and 2020.

Sanders was a threat to the status quo, as well as corporate America's vast profits that go along with it. He wanted to bring the working class together to fight for a government that worked for all of us, not just a select few. The top 1 percent of this country, with the owners of the mainstream media among them, didn't like this, so they made it their objective to try and shut down Sanders, both in 2016 and 2020. They did this by making a concentrated effort not to cover him, and when they did cover him, the coverage was negative more often than it was positive.

The financial elites overwhelmingly support establishment politicians, because they aren't a threat to their profits. It's

---

187 *David Rutz,* "Ed Schultz Suggests MSNBC Fired Him Because of Bernie Sanders Support," April 16, 2018, video, 8:59.

why the mainstream media favored Hillary Clinton in 2016. Clinton had taken big-money campaign contributions from billionaires, including Mark Cuban, Michael Bloomberg, Meg Whitman, and Warren Buffet.[188] Her biggest billionaire donor was hedge funder George Soros. He contributed more than eleven million dollars.[189] She also received donations from Alice Walton, the heiress to the Walmart fortune, as well as James Simmons, another hedge fund manager.[190] Clinton was also the beneficiary of fundraisers held by Comcast executives, the parent company of MSNBC and NBC.[191] She had the support of big money, and because of this, the mainstream media supported her and did everything they could to make sure she received the Democratic nomination.

Ed Schultz definitely thought the mainstream media was in favor of Clinton.

"I think the Clintons were connected to Andy Lack, connected at the hip," Schultz said. "I think that they didn't want anybody in their prime time or anywhere in their lineup supporting Bernie Sanders. I think that they were in the tank for Hillary Clinton and I think it was managed, and forty-five days later, I was out at MSNBC." [192]

---

188 Alicia Adamczyk, "More Billionaires Are Donating to Hillary Clinton Than Donald Trump," *Money*, September 26, 2016.

189 Ibid.

190 Ibid.

191 Dan Norton, "Comcast Exec to Hold Fundraiser for Hillary Clinton," *Philadelphia Business Journal*, updated June 12, 2015.

192 Rutz, "Ed Schultz Suggests."

Andrew Lack, who Schultz is referring to, was the executive chairman of NBC News and MSNBC.

"But the fact of the matter is, I think I've got a hell of a story to tell and when you see how the campaign unfolded, Donna Brazile feeding Hillary Clinton questions at the campaign, the DNC undercutting Bernie Sanders, the superdelegates that were organized by Hillary Clinton, I mean, in my state of Minnesota, where I'm a resident and pay taxes, Al Franken and Amy Klobuchar were superdelegates and despite the fact that Bernie Sanders won Minnesota, they supported Clinton. It was that the fix was in. The fix was in with the mainstream media, the fix was in with managing the news and shutting down Bernie Sanders, and it wasn't until he started matching the Clintons and raising money that he became 'well, we gotta cover this guy.' [193]

"But from the start, the Clintons didn't want any competition, they didn't want Bernie Sanders around, they didn't want the Keystone XL pipeline, they didn't want to push her on that issue, they didn't want to push her on free education for all, and they certainly didn't want to push her on the TPP, and also universal healthcare. Those were four main issues that, had Bernie Sanders not been in the campaign, Hillary Clinton would have never had to address, and so I think the fix was in early on to deep-six Bernie. To this day, it kind of pisses me off, because, you know, they talk about collusion, there's [no more] collusion than this."[194]

---

193 Ibid.

194 Ibid.

Schultz laid out a good case. Now that's just his opinion, but hey, I can't say I don't believe him. A network owned by a billion-dollar corporation, and one that has corporate executives who hold fundraisers for Hillary Clinton, doesn't want the guy running against Clinton and who wants to redistribute wealth to be president?[195] A network that receives loads of money in advertising dollars from private health insurance companies doesn't want the guy who wants to outlaw private health insurance and provide Medicare-for-all to be president? It all seems pretty believable to me, and Schultz isn't the only one who has stories to share about the mainstream media's support for Clinton and disdain for Sanders.

Krystal Ball is a former MSNBC host and is now the cohost of *Rising with Krystal & Saagar*, an ever-growing alternative news program that is produced by *The Hill*. Ball was the co-host of the MSNBC show *The Cycle* when she did a segment that wasn't in line with the network's standards of how to treat Hillary Clinton. On an episode of *Rising*, she told the story of how she pleaded for Hillary Clinton not to run on air, and what followed because of the words she spoke on air.

"Back in early 2015 at MSNBC, I did a monologue that some of you may have seen, pretty much begging Hillary Clinton not to run," Ball stated. "I said her elite ties were out of step with the party and the country, that if she ran, she would likely be the nominee and would then go on to lose. No one censored me, I was allowed to say it, but afterward, the Clinton people called and complained to the MSNBC top brass and threatened not to provide any access during the

---

195 Norton, "Comcast Exec to Hold Fundraiser for Hillary Clinton."

upcoming campaign. I was told that I could still say what I wanted, but I would have to get any Clinton-related commentary cleared with the president of the network. Now being a human interested in maintaining my job, I'm certain I did less critical Clinton commentary after that then I maybe otherwise would have." [196]

Ball had Clinton-related coverage censored, and that's all you need to know. MSNBC, along with the rest of the mainstream media, was in support of Clinton over Sanders in 2016 because she wasn't a threat to their owners' pockets, whereas Sanders was. Ball went on to further detail why the media was anti-Bernie.

"Every journalist at every outlet knows what they can say and do freely and what's going to be a little stickier," Ball said. "No one is ever going to have their anti-Bernie pieces called in to question since he stands outside the system. Their invites to the DC establishment world are not going to be revoked, and may even be heightened by negative Bernie coverage." [197]

The media was much more favorable to Clinton than Sanders in 2016. This dynamic only continued into the 2020 Democratic primaries. Unlike in 2016, when Sanders had virtually no name recognition outside of his home state of Vermont, Sanders was a national figure entering the race for the 2020 Democratic nomination for president. He was the most popular senator in the country, so he had a real shot to win the

---

196 Caitlin Johnstone, "Former MSNBC Reporter Spills Details on Pro-establishment Bias in Media," *Caitlin Johnstone*, August 15, 2019.

197 Ibid.

Democratic nomination.[198] [199] However, the mainstream media would never admit to that and would hardly even talk about him. When they would, they would dismiss him and blatantly lie about him.

It started right away, and continued all the way throughout the primary. In the week of Sanders's campaign launch, Zerlina Maxwell, a former Hillary Clinton campaign staffer, was brought on MSNBC and introduced as an MSNBC analyst. She was allowed to falsely accuse Sanders of not mentioning race or gender until twenty-three minutes into his launch speech.[200] In July, an MSNBC legal analyst claimed Bernie Sanders made her skin crawl, and she couldn't even explain why.[201] There were many uncalled-for comments like this throughout the campaign. MSNBC anchor Chuck Todd read an article on air relating Sanders supporters to a "digital brownshirt brigade." [202]

Former MSNBC host Chris Matthews had an even crazier rant when he related Sanders to public executions. After the

---

198 John Bowden, "Poll: Sanders Most Popular Senator, Flake Least," *The Hill*, January 10, 2019.

199 Zack Budryk, "Sanders, Klobuchar among Five Most Popular Senators: Poll," *The Hill*, April 25, 2019.

200 Glenn Greenwald, "MSNBC Yet Again Broadcasts Blatant Lies, This Time about Bernie Sanders's Opening Speech, and Refuses to Correct Them," *The Intercept*, March 3, 2019.

201 Katie Halper, "MSNBC's Anti-sanders Bias Makes It Forget How to Do Math," *Fair*, July 26, 2019.

202 Ian Schwartz, "Chuck Todd Cites Quote Calling Sanders Supporters 'Digital Brownshirt Brigade,'" *RealClear Politics*, February 10, 2020.

February 7, 2020, Democratic debate in New Hampshire, Chris Matthews was part of an MSNBC panel for post-debate coverage. Matthews held nothing back when discussing his thoughts on Sanders.[203]

Matthews started his rant by saying he'd keep his opinions on socialism to himself, but then in the same breath, he contradicted himself and started sharing.

"I have my own views of the word 'socialist,' and I'd be glad to share them with you in private. They go back to the early 1950s. I have an attitude about them. I remember the Cold War," Matthews said.[204]

"I have an attitude toward [Fidel] Castro," he continued. "I believe if Castro and the Reds had won the Cold War, there would have been executions in Central Park, and I might have been one of the ones getting executed, and certain other people would be there cheering, okay?" [205]

Matthews then went on to connect Sanders to the executions.

"So, I have a problem with people who take the other side. I don't know who Bernie supports over these years," Matthews said. "I don't know what he means by socialist. One week it's Denmark. We're going to be like Denmark. Okay, that's

203 Peter Wade, "Chris Matthews' Wild Rant Connects a Bernie Sanders Win with Public Executions," *RollingStone*, February 8, 2020.
204 Ibid.
205 Ibid.

harmless, that's basically a capitalist country with a lot of good social welfare programs. Denmark is harmless." [206]

Matthews' cohost, Chris Hayes, fortunately defended Sanders by saying he's pretty obviously in the Denmark category, which is 100 percent correct.

Matthews still wasn't having it and questioned Hayes' comment.

"Is he? How do you know? Did he tell you that?" Matthews questioned. [207]

Two possibilities could have been the cause of this rant. The first being Matthews just couldn't stand the thought of a Sanders presidency, because he would be a threat to the status quo Matthews has benefitted so much from. So, in turn, Matthews was trying to thrash Sanders's momentum and do anything he could to kneecap him. The other option is Matthews really is that ignorant of who Sanders is and what he's all about. Maybe he hasn't bothered to really learn about Sanders and everything he knows comes from people inside his bubble who are opposed to Sanders's policies. So which one is it? It's probably a mix of both. Matthews isn't a total idiot, even though he is extremely out of touch because he lives and works in a bubble. He's also a multimillionaire, having a net worth of somewhere around twenty million

---

206 Ibid.
207 Ibid.

dollars.[208] He knew Sanders wanted to redistribute the wealth in the United States and make the country a fairer and more equitable place for everyone, not just people like Matthews. It's fair to say Matthews didn't want that.

There were many instances of obvious anti-Sanders coverage in the mainstream media throughout the campaign. It wasn't exclusively MSNBC who tried to prevent Sanders from winning the nomination.

The Jeff Bezos-owned *Washington Post* once ran sixteen negative stories about Sanders in sixteen hours.[209] Fox News once ran a headline of "Biden rebound continues. Warren falls to third," and accompanied it with a picture of Biden, Warren, and Buttigieg, noticeably excluding second place Sanders from the story.[210] CNN went with a headline that ignored the fact Sanders was in second place, within the margin of error for the lead, so he was statistically tied for first. The headline instead emphasized Buttigieg and Biden were polling close to first place. The headline read as "Iowa poll: Biden and Buttigieg Within Striking Distance of Warren." The results of the poll had Warren at 22 percent, Sanders at 19, Buttigieg at 18, and Biden at 17.[211] CBS once removed Sanders completely from a graphic titled "Top Picks for Democratic

---

208 "Chris Matthews Net Worth," *Celebrity Net Worth*, accessed January 25, 2021.

209 Julie Hollar, "Here's the Evidence Corporate Media Say Is Missing of Wapo Bias against Sanders," *Fair*, August 15, 2019.

210 Nolan Higdon and Mickey Huff, "The Bernie Blackout Is Real, and These Screenshots Prove It," *Truthout*, January 30, 2020.

211 Ibid.

Nominee Among New Hampshire Primary Voters." Sanders was among the top three, but the graphic didn't show him. It showed Warren instead.[212] These were all deliberate attempts to hinder the Sanders campaign.

"I think the media, the political press, certainly during the primary had an eye-rolling attitude toward Bernie and the politics he promotes," David Sirota, a senior advisor and speechwriter on the Sanders campaign, told me.

Sanders was able to persevere through the media's attempts to derail his campaign. They tried to erase him by simply not covering his campaign, then when that didn't work, they tried to attack him and claim he was unelectable. Yet the Sanders campaign was able to fight through it all and managed to still be a real contender.

Sirota said they tried to stick to their message and not get sucked into all the frivolous stories the media tried to churn up.

"Political coverage often tends to be infotainment rather than focusing on the issues, so I think we did a good job of not getting sucked into that," Sirota said. "I think we focused on building out a communications infrastructure that tried to speak directly to voters, as opposed to only through media intermediaries, and I think that when necessary, we tried to call out some of the unfair coverage that we received."

---

212 Ibid.

Sanders and his campaign fought through all the attempts to stall his campaign in route to winning the first three primaries and caucuses. Iowa was disputed because Pete Buttigieg emerged with a hair more state delegate equivalents, but Sanders won the raw vote by over six thousand votes. Sanders was the winner, but the media just tried to spin it like he wasn't in order to prevent him from gaining any momentum. After the shitshow that was the Iowa caucuses, Sanders won the New Hampshire primary and the Nevada caucus. He was the overwhelming frontrunner, but the mainstream media wouldn't give him his due. Instead, they attacked him and tried to lift up his opponents in any way they could.

Ultimately, the Democratic establishment and mainstream media ganged up and threw their support behind Joe Biden in order to stop Sanders from winning the nomination. It worked, as Biden went on to secure the party's nomination thanks to the wave of support he received from the mainstream media.

"I think that the tenor of media coverage was not helpful in general to our campaign, while it was helpful to other campaigns," Sirota said. "Bernie won the first three caucuses and primaries. I know Iowa is in dispute, but he certainly won the most votes there, and he was not afforded the kind of positive momentum coverage that Joe Biden was rewarded with after Biden won South Carolina. I think there was a study done that found that Biden got something like eighty million dollars' equivalence of positive media coverage after winning one primary. We didn't benefit from that when Bernie won New Hampshire or Nevada, so I think there was certainly evidence that there were two sets of standards, one for Bernie and one for everyone else in terms of the coverage. Now is that the reason we didn't win the race? I wouldn't say that there was any one singular reason, but certainly, I would say that we faced headwinds."

Sirota is correct in his assessment of how the race went. When he makes note of the positive momentum coverage Biden received, he's referring to data published by the media tracking service Critical Mention that noted between the time polls closed in South Carolina and Super Tuesday, Biden received an estimated twenty-two million dollars in media coverage.[213]

Another study on media coverage in the race, published by *In These Times*, found in its August and September 2019 coverage MSNBC talked about Biden three times more than they spoke about Sanders, and the coverage Sanders did get was far more negative than that of his opponents.[214]

This opposition to Sanders from the mainstream media, along with establishment candidates lining up behind Biden, propelled Biden past Sanders and ensured the status quo of our country would not be altered.

"I think that the corporate-owned media tends to be much more of a defender of the status quo and a purveyor of policies that protect that status quo than they are interested in

---

213 Caleb Ecarma, "Joe Biden, Revenant, Was an Irresistible Media Story— and It Helped Win Him Super Tuesday," *Vanity Fair*, March 5, 2020.

214 Luke Savage, "The Corporate Media's War against Bernie Sanders Is Very Real," *Jacobin*, November 20, 2019.

policies that would change the system, and certainly policies that could end up redistributing wealth to the middle class as opposed to the system that continues to distribute income up the income ladder," Sirota exclaimed.

The mainstream media uses its power to dictate elections. This results in a politics that serves corporate interests, not the American people. What happened to the Sanders's campaigns of 2016 and 2020 is a great example of this, but it's important to remember he is not alone in this. Other candidates have been deemed as threats to the system as well, and have had the power of the corporate media thrown at them as well.

Andrew Yang saw this happen to him as well in the 2020 primary season. He was somebody who was viewed as an outsider, supporting policies like Medicare-for-all and a universal basic income. In response to this, he faced similar obstacles to Sanders. The mainstream media didn't give him a fair shake. He wasn't given an equal amount of speaking time in the debates, and MSNBC would frequently make mistakes when covering him, including getting his name wrong in graphics. They once referred to him as John Yang in a graphic on air.[215] This stuff never happened to the corporate-friendly candidates like Biden, Harris, and Buttigieg.

The mainstream media holds a tremendous amount of power in sculpting our nation's politics. This power is why billionaires and top-of-the-line corporations have been buying

---

215 Nicholas Wu, "'John Yang?' Andrew Yang Pokes Fun at MSNBC for Flubbing His Name in Broadcast," *USA Today*, September 10, 2019.

up the media in our country. They use the media to their advantage by raising up establishment politicians like President Biden while crushing champions of the working class and threats to their power and profits, like Bernie Sanders. If Americans are going to have a government that works for them, they need a press that works for them. Until that happens, we can't expect much help from the politicians in Washington.

PART 4

FIXING THE NEWS

CHAPTER 9

THE FIX

———

To this point, this book has been quite depressing. It's been depressing to write, and I'm sure it's been depressing to read. Our future, though, does not have to be depressing. We can change the structure of corporate ownership that is holding our journalists hostage. We can get a truly free press, a press that tells the truth and only the truth no matter what, a true fourth estate.

Today our journalists are held captive by the incentive structure that is in place at the mainstream news outlets of this country. It's not the individual journalist's fault our news lacks objectivity and wholesomeness. Journalists must comply with what their editors and/or executive producers want, the editors must comply with what the executives at the networks desire, and they must comply with what their corporate owners want. This chain of command leads to the interests of the corporate owners shining through in our 'news.'

The vast majority of journalists enter the profession for the right reasons; they want to serve the public by holding the powerful accountable. They want to be hard-hitting, objective journalists, but the current system leads them astray. They know in order to keep their jobs and be in line for promotions, they must follow their editors' and producers' directions. The system impels journalists with corporate-friendly beliefs up the ranks, while those who stand up for the working class are left behind. Therefore, journalists who may actually support working-class causes are incentivized to stay quiet and report the news through a corporate-friendly perspective. Most of them do, and those who don't get thrown out of the mainstream media altogether.

The bottom line is the quality and reliability of journalism is hurting in this country, and the reason for this is the structure of corporate ownership. In order to get a press that is truly working for us and not just corporate America, we must strip corporate America of its influence completely. We do this by first calling out the mainstream media for what it is, a tool for corporate America to sculpt public opinion in a manner that is beneficial to them, and second, by abandoning them in favor of alternatives that utilize a different incentive structure. We must support and get our news from independent media outlets who rely on their viewers for funding, and are thereby beholden to their viewers.

Cenk Uygur has been trying to implement this exact type of incentive structure at his media company, The Young Turks. He described this new type of incentive structure and why it's a requirement if you want to have good, solid, reliable news.

"There's none of that BS corporate pressure, etc., because if you think about it logically, even if we wanted to do that, all that would do is ruin [TYT's] brand," Uygur said. "What I tried to do, knowing all these factors to varying degrees throughout these eighteen years that we've been doing it, is set up the incentive structure so that this company will naturally do the right thing even if I'm not here. So, first of all, you have to be ever vigilant. So, I'm vigilant as I run the company to not get sucked up into short-term interests, or financial interests, let's put it that way. Long-term is more important, which is create an incentive system that rewards you if you are good to the audience, if you serve the audience.

"So, how do you do that?" Uygur continued. "By relying on subscription more and audience funding. So, people misunderstand it sometimes, and I understand why. They say, 'Oh, you know, you guys just keep asking your audience for money.' Yes, but think about why. It's actually a really uncomfortable thing to do, and we don't like doing it, and I can't stand it. Other hosts are understandably bothered by it because it's not a natural human instinct to keep asking people for money. But the reason why I insist on it is because that then means we're connected to the audience, that's who our boss is. So, if MSNBC betrays Clorox, there's going to be a price to pay; if we betray the audience, then there's a price to pay. So, then I've lined up my incentives with serving our audience."

The mainstream media outlets have allegiances to their advertisers and their corporate owners. Uygur is describing this phenomenon using Clorox and MSNBC as an example. The idea is media outlets won't report on things that portray their advertisers in a negative light because they don't want to lose the revenue that comes from said advertisers. Some of the companies that pay money to advertise on the cable news networks include Nutrisystem, Otezla, Sleep Number, Liberty Mutual, T-Mobile, GEICO, Progressive, GoodRx, Trivago, Office Depot, Cadillac, Proactive, Verizon, and ClearChoice.[216] This is not a comprehensive list by any means, but you can start to get the picture. Relying on these corporate advertisers, as well as their direct corporate owners for your operating costs, opens up the newsrooms to bias. They care more about serving their owners and advertisers than their viewers and readers.

So how do we fix that? We change the structure of news in our country to a structure that incentivizes serving the audience first and foremost by reporting objective, wholesome news without the corporate bias. As Uygur said, create a system where the audience is the boss. He further detailed how this system looks, mentioning how this could save the mainstream media outlets in our country, and gave a good example by way of the *New York Times*.

"The bottom line is there is a better way to do media," Uygur stated. "It's harder, but it's better to be as close to the audience as you can. By the way, this could rescue the establishment media. It's already having an impact on the *New York Times*, although it's so slow and the old culture is very hard to uproot. So, for example, when two-thirds of *New York Times'* revenue came from advertising and Miramax (Harvey Weinstein's company) was a giant advertiser for the *New York Times*, they had the Harvey Weinstein story and they didn't

---

216 Chris Ariens, "Here Are the Biggest Advertisers on Fox News, CNN and MSNBC," *TVNewser*, March 9, 2018.

run it, and then when two-thirds of their money came from subscription, they then ran the Harvey Weinstein story. So, they'll say it was a coincidence, I'll say coincidence, my ass. That's not remotely a coincidence. It's not conspiratorial, it's just the invisible hand of the market. And so, if you realize that the invisible hand of the market exists, well, then set up an incentive structure that will get you better results and have you deliver for the audience.

"The reason why people don't do it is because it's really hard," Uygur continued. "I know so many digital media companies that are in the same situation we are and they just go grab millions of dollars from the Lockheed Martins of the world and then investors yell at me like, 'Why don't you just do what they're doing? It's so easy, just go get the millions of dollars. You know you're doing this long, hard trek of trying to, you know, create the right incentive structure, just get the money from Lockheed Martin.' That's just the wrong way to go about it, obviously."

The invisible hand of the market certainly does exist. Money is a necessity in today's world, so we really can't fault people or media outlets for doing whatever it takes to make money. What we can do is educate ourselves on the effects the invisible hand of the market has on our news today (hint, it's a harmful one). We can then use that education to make the informed choice to forego getting our news from mainstream media outlets who utilize incentive structures that promote serving corporate interests, and instead get our news from independent media outlets who utilize incentive structures that promote serving the interests of their audience, or the American people.

When media outlets rely on their audience for funding, as in subscriptions or other forms of audience funding, they are forced to continue to provide high-quality journalism. If they don't, their viewers or readers will unsubscribe, the company will lose their funding, and they will go out of business while their viewers find another source that is doing a better job. This structure also allows for journalists to report the truth no matter what it is. They don't have to censor certain information in order to not reflect poorly on their corporate owners and advertisers.

Under the current structure, the most important aspect isn't the audience, because losing viewers isn't the biggest threat to their funding. Losing advertisers is a bigger concern, and the biggest concern of all is not pushing their parent companies' agendas. From getting government approval on mergers to the lowering of corporate taxes, Comcast, AT&T, The Walt Disney Company, Fox Corporation, and ViacomCBS all have their desires and they all rank above audience satisfaction with their news coverage. The same applies to Jeff Bezos and his *Washington Post*.

"A lot of this goes back to a monopolized society and culture and industry," David Sirota told me. "I mean, [the media conglomerates] aren't technically monopolies, but there's certainly an oligopoly that controls and patrols the terms of the political debate in America. My book *Hostile Takeover*, you know, one of the underlying premises of the book was that if you can control the terms of the political debate, you don't have to attach yourself to envelopes that buy votes on the floor of Congress. That if you capture, fully capture, the American political system and the political debate, then you don't need petty corruption to get things done. If you're a corporation and you don't care if it's between the outcome of option A and option B, but you really don't want outcome C, you can narrow the discussion between the parties to just A and B, then you don't care who wins. No one's talking about C; C's got no chance."

This is what the mainstream media is incentivized to do. Their goal is to shape the political debate, much more so than it is to serve their audience, the American people.

Our news would be of much higher quality and much more reliable if we ditched the current structure of corporate ownership for an independent, subscriber-funded structure. However, it is also important to make sure there is a large variety of sources to report the news. If we have only one outlet that is independent of corporate interests and it grows to be a massive company, it may not be representative of all the viewpoints and life experiences we have in our country. We need many, smaller in scale, independent media outlets to have a truly successful media dynamic in this country.

David Sirota wholeheartedly agrees with this notion. He elaborated on his thoughts in his conversation with me as well.

"I think we have a problem in the media industry of bigness," Sirota said. "Size has been a big part of the problem. Our generation is so used to these huge corporate media conglomerates, but it hasn't always been that way in America. In the era of the penny press and the pamphlets, now I mean, people roll their eyes and say that's old fashioned, but I think it's much healthier for democracy when there are a lot of small and medium-sized media outlets competing with each other, and that we don't need a system that is controlled by such a small group of people.

"I mean, *The Note* on ABC, when I was, you know, twenty years ago, working on Capitol Hill, *The Note* billed itself as a newsletter for the five hundred people in Washington who make decisions for the rest of the country, so media, the politicos, etc. I think it was inadvertently diagnosing the inherent oligarchic structure of our society, government, and culture. That really there shouldn't be five hundred people in offices in Washington controlling everything in our media and our politics.

"You know what gives me hope is I'm not aspiring, in my own work, to be some huge media mogul. I want to do my work, I want to hire some journalists, do some good work, and contribute to a more vibrant democracy, but, like, I don't have dreams of being some mogul. By that I don't mean that I'm saying I'm a martyr, but that's not the vision of a healthy democracy that I see. I think that twenty years from now, if you told me that, yeah, you know there were a couple more huge cable outlets that came along and their owners were somewhat more progressive, or you give me a choice of where there's a lot of medium-sized media outlets and there was real competition, a real vibrancy of viewpoints, you know, I'd say, I'd say I'd choose the latter option."

Sirota is right. A larger number of smaller media outlets is preferable to a smaller number of larger media outlets. Even if one or two independent networks grew to be as big or bigger than the cable networks, which it looks like some like

TYT will, it still wouldn't be the best thing for journalism. It'd be a great development and much better than what we currently have, but it wouldn't be perfect. One independent media outlet is much easier to corrupt than many independent media outlets.

In a landscape where there are many independent media outlets, if one gets corrupted and goes and takes big money from massive corporations, similar to the fashion Uygur described, their quality of news would suffer. Since there are many more independent outlets, the people would be able to reject the outlet that went corporate and relinquish watching them. This fear of losing their audience would incentivize independent outlets to stay independent and refrain from taking big money. Many small to medium-sized independent networks insulate the new incentive structure from being hijacked by corporations.

Another benefit to having a large number of smaller independent news organizations is they can be more local. With more outlets, they can be located in cities and states across our country. We have that now, but the local stations and newspapers are also not independent from big corporations, and hence they lack objectivity as well. The ability to be more local is a compelling reason in favor of multiple independent outlets because local news teams always do a better job than national news teams when covering local stories. The reason for this: they actually live in the area. They have the same lived experiences as their audience, and this leads to a much better understanding of local happenings. This is just another justification for a large number of smaller in size, independent, subscriber-funded media outlets

We need to shift our media landscape to one that incentivizes media outlets to be beholden to their audience. The way we do this is by calling out the corporate-owned mainstream media and abandoning them for independent outlets that are funded through means of audience funding. It connects them to their audience and promotes a much higher quality of journalism. We also need many of these independent outlets to ensure a vibrant flow of ideas, that all voices can participate and be heard, as well as to prevent corporate interests or the wealthy elite from being able to hijack this new structure. This is achievable, and there are already numerous independent outlets out there. All we have to do is start supporting them and treating them as our main sources of information, not the corporately owned mainstream media.

CHAPTER 10

WHERE TO TURN
PART 1

—

If you've made it this far, you're probably wondering where to look. You may be telling yourself, "Sure, I get it, the mainstream media isn't objective, their end goal is to benefit their corporate owners, not tell me the truth. I can stop watching them, but getting the news is important to me, so where should I turn?"

You're right, it can be confusing, especially if this is new information. So where should you turn to get your news? I wish I could say just watch your local news and read your local papers, but sadly, the corporate world has gotten to them as well.

Big-monied venture capitalists are buying up smaller local papers all across the country and depleting them of their resources just to make a quick buck.

Dave Krieger has been a journalist in Colorado since 1981. He was the editorial page editor for the Boulder *Daily Camera* from November 2014 to April 2018. In a TEDx Talk Boulder talk titled "Who Owns the News?," Krieger told the story of how he was fired for self-publishing a story that was killed by the paper's owner. The story described how the paper's owner, Alden Global Capital, was draining the business of cash and putting the paper's existence at risk.

"So, as you may have heard, the *Daily Camera* editorial page was recently censored," Krieger told the audience.[217]

"On orders from its parent company, an editorial warning about a threat to its existence was killed. The editorial criticized the owner of the *Camera*, which is a hedge fund in New York City, for draining the business of cash at such an aggressive rate that the survival of the newspaper is now in doubt." [218]

Krieger went on to describe what the story said and the business model that was killing the *Daily Camera*.

"It pointed out that this particular hedge fund, Alden Global Capital, has as its business model, taking exorbitant profits out of businesses that have declining revenues as it is. This resembles nothing quite so much as a mob protection racket. These, uh, corporate enforcers show up at the businesses, they take their cut off the top, 20 percent of gross revenues more

---

217 *TedX Talks*, "Who Owns the News?," June 26, 2018, video, 17:22.
218 Ibid.

or less, then they zoom out again, and they leave the local managers to figure out how to keep the lights on." [219]

"Well, if your business is suffering declining revenues year after year after year, the only way you're going to do that is to cut, cut, cut, and that's why the *Daily Camera* and its staff along with the *Denver Post*, the *Orange County California Register*, the *St. Paul MN Pioneer Press*, the *San Jose Mercury News*, the *Boston Herald*, and dozens and dozens of other daily newspapers in our country keep getting smaller and smaller with every year." [220]

Sadly, it seems as if our once reliable local papers are now falling victim to corporate interests, just like the mainstream outlets. Krieger went into further detail about what was happening at the paper.

"It was a former news editor at the *Denver Post* who put this more succinctly, as he was resigning. He said the post is, quote, 'being murdered by its owners now,'" Krieger said. "The hedge funds, and there's other hedge funds than Alden, that are involved in this distressed asset business, they say they're just basically like every other newspaper owner. Revenues are declining, and therefore, cuts have to be made. But that disguises the actual fact that there are newspapers where the owners are taking much more modest profit levels and reinvesting the difference in new revenue streams, trying to

---

219 Ibid.
220 Ibid.

cobble together a sustainable new business model for these journalistic enterprises. [221]

"What the hedge fund does of course, is quite the opposite. They call these people vulture capitalists for a reason. Their business model has nothing to do with sustainable or long-term growth. Their business model is specifically to drain as much cash as possible, as quickly as possible, from the distressed asset and then move on to the next one, often leaving little more than a carcass behind." [222]

Krieger said this process is like a con game that preys on the subscriber. He said the product, the newspaper itself, declines, and subscription costs rise. They use the loyalty of the long-term customer against them to maximize their profits. The goal of the news is no longer to inform the people and play the role of watchdog. Instead, it is just to maximize profits for its owners at the mainstream media outlets and local media outlets.

This story also serves as another prime example of censorship in the news. Krieger described how so in his talk as well.

"As the community storyteller, the *Daily Camera* would have been obliged to tell this story about any other 128-year-old local institution that was suddenly on the verge of collapse," Krieger said. "In this case, because the story was about the paper itself, and because its owners are, shall we say, publicity-shy, the *Daily Camera* was prohibited from telling this

---

221 Ibid.

222 Ibid.

story, and in that process, the traditional wall between the journalism enterprise and the business enterprise that is sacred to reputable journalism organizations everywhere was demolished. [223]

"The business side of the *Daily Camera* essentially invaded the editorial side and started determining what could be published and what could not based on the business interests of the owners." [224]

In response to this censorship, Krieger did what any good journalist should do. He still got the story out. He self-published the censored editorial online, and was promptly fired by the *Daily Camera* for doing so.

"The Editorial Advisory Board at the *Camera*, which is a group of local residents that write to the paper once a week, collaborated on an essay protesting both the censorship and the firing," Krieger said. "The *Daily Camera* refused to publish that as well. So, these were acts of censorship by the shadow forces that now control many, many American daily newspapers across the country." [225]

This story simply states our local media is being corrupted as well, so abandoning the mainstream media just to turn to the present-day local media wouldn't be the most successful plan of action.

---

223 Ibid.
224 Ibid.
225 Ibid.

So, this begs the question again, where can we turn to get honest and objective reporting? Fortunately, there are some options out there.

CHAPTER 10

WHERE TO TURN PART 2

———

So where do we turn to get honest and objective reporting? Fortunately for us, there are some options out there currently. There is a growing number of alternative news outlets popping up across the country that do a much better job of providing a well-balanced, complete, and objective version of what is going on in the world. They are structured in different ways than the mainstream media, which allows them to maintain freedom in their reporting.

I will detail some of them, but there are many out there, and I strongly advise you to search for yourself.

THE YOUNG TURKS

The Young Turks was founded in 2002 as a radio talk show on Sirius Satellite Radio by Cenk Uygur. As I've previously mentioned, he turned down a radio-only deal worth two hundred fifty thousand dollars in 2006 in favor of becoming the first online talk show to stream daily.[226] Fast forward fourteen years and the decision Uygur made has turned out to be the right one. Uygur has stuck with TYT and built an entire network around his flagship show *The Young Turks*. The TYT network now has two hundred million views a month and seven billion total views.[227]

TYT has grown to where it is today in large part due to their authenticity. They deem themselves "the home of progressives," and they are overwhelmingly progressive. Some may view taking a strong political stance as a bad thing, and that it may be detrimental to reporting the news objectively. However, TYT doing this actually has the exact opposite effect.

The viewer knows what the hosts' opinions are, so they are more able to distinguish between an opinion and a fact. It also establishes more credibility because they are being honest. It doesn't help the mainstream media when they blatantly lie by claiming they're objective, unbiased news sources. It just hurts their credibility and makes people ponder what else they may be lying about. The hosts at TYT are honest about their beliefs and do a very good job of separating facts and opinions. They never give you an opinion disguised as facts, something the mainstream media does all the time. TYT's up-front honesty about their political views establishes credibility and makes them more trustworthy.

---

226 Chavala Madlena, "Cenk Uygur on the Success of the Young Turks," *The Guardian*, April 26, 2010.

227 "TYT Network," *TOPIO Networks*," accessed January 25, 2020.

They are also a more reliable source than those of the mainstream media because they aren't owned and operated by corporate America. In fact, corporate America and the mainstream media hate Uygur; just look at the reactions to his congressional run in the 2020 special primary election to fill former representative of California's 25th congressional district Katie Hill's seat. They did everything they could to smear him and prevent his campaign from winning, even going as far as suggesting Uygur defended the former Ku Klux Klan leader David Duke, which was an appalling lie. [228]

Why do they hate him? Well, it's because he and TYT are trying to change the system and stand up for working-class people. I've previously stated how in order to get a news media that serves the American people and not just big corporate and establishment interests, we must change the structure of our media system in this country. Uygur and TYT are doing just that, and that's why the mainstream media and their corporate owners hate him.

TYT is connected to their audience, because rather than being bankrolled by big corporations or billionaires like Jeff Bezos, TYT is bankrolled by their audience. They rely on subscriptions and donations for the vast majority of their funding. This incentivizes them to continue to provide high-quality journalism because if they don't, or they start lying or getting things wrong, they will go out of business. It's a risk that just isn't there in the mainstream media, and

---

228 Joseph Wulfsohn, "New York Times Issues Correction after Suggesting Cenk Uygur Defended David Duke," *Fox News*, December 17, 2019.

it's why TYT does a much better job of reporting the news than the mainstream outlets.

TYT is growing and will soon surpass the mainstream media as they are dominant with younger viewers, whereas the mainstream relies more on older demographics.[229] Uygur laid this entire dynamic out and detailed how he and TYT plan to surpass the mainstream media outlets in this country.

"There's really three buckets," Uygur stated. "There's old TV, so the traditional twenty-four-hour cable news channel and the money that you make from that, where the CNN's of the world are dominant, but now the OTTs (Over The Tops, a term used for delivering film and TV content over the Internet) are in that bucket. We're on more than half a dozen platforms—Roku, Pluto, XUMO, Comcast Xfinity, Samsung, YouTube TV, and more on the way. So, if you watch on those new OTTs, there's very little difference between TYT and CNN, so we're in the same ball game and we're in the same market, but in that bucket, TV's still super dominant. So, they have the overwhelming majority of the audience.

"Then there's this second bucket which is kind of an oddball. It's what's called your O&O's, your owned and operated, so that's your website, your apps, and anything along those lines. So that's where, again, the CNN's of the world do really well, because they have a very strong brand, they have a ton of money, and they can drive people to their website.

---

229 226 Eric Blattberg, "The Young Turks Is Running Circles around News Networks on YouTube," *DigDay*, October 31, 2014.

"So then there's a third bucket, which is the present and the future; that's social media: Facebook, YouTube, Twitch, Twitter, etc., and in social media, we're dominant. We're top five in every platform, we're number two on Facebook, above CNN, Fox News, MSNBC, etc. Among the young, we crush. Under twenty-four-year-olds, we beat CNN, MSNBC, and Fox News combined.

"So we own the future. You explain that to people, they logically get it, but they can't believe it. They just keep thinking, 'Yeah, yeah, but you're TYT and they're CNN, it's not going to happen,' but they're wrong. It's already happening. I started in my living room, no connections, no money, no nothing, and here I am. In June, we had 524 million views. None of it is bought; all of it is organic, half a billion views a month, so this is a steam roller."

Uygur went on to lay out his vision for how his media company he started in his living room may one day become the biggest in the world.

"So, let me tell you how the future is going to work. Number one, we're going to keep expanding our lead in social media, and if we do it right, we will be so dominant in social media they will feel suffocated. Then the next thing that is going to happen is, they're stuck on cable news, they can't get off it because the subscriber fees are so much and such a big part of their revenue that they can't leave, and that means that they can't put their original programming online, they can only do some clips and they're contractually prohibited from doing more. Well, that means they're just giving me the future, just giving it to me, so I'm going to take it. Then, eventually, our twenty-four-hour channels are going to be bigger than theirs, and then where does that leave us? If I'm right about all of this, or maybe even some of this, as the number one media company in the world when it comes to news, and that is that."

TYT may not become the biggest news media company on the planet, but it is on track to surge past the CNN's, MSN-BC's, and FOX News' of the world. That is a great thing for the future of our news because TYT does a much better job of reporting the news in an objective fashion than the mainstream due to the incentive structure Uygur has been so deliberate in setting up.

If we get a press that represents us and not just the corporate elites of this county, one can assume TYT will have a large role in that. Even if you don't identify as a progressive, I highly suggest checking out TYT, because they are much more objective than the mainstream networks, and you will be much better off because of that. You can find TYT programming on YouTube, their website tyt.com, and select streaming platforms.

RISING

TYT is not the only up-and-coming alternative news source out there with an MSNBC outcast as its co-anchor. *The Hill's Rising with Krystal & Saagar* is an online morning news show produced by *The Hill* and cohosted by Krystal Ball and Saagar Enjeti. The show is filmed on weekdays and can be found on YouTube and *The Hill's* website.

Enjeti is a conservative, and Ball is a progressive, so that in itself leads to a good variety of ideas and stories covered on the show: a relief to those who are sick of one-sided mainstream media programming, where they will only give a fair shot to those on their side. Whether it be Fox News with Republicans or MSNBC with Democrats, it's really one and the same; and to be clear, the mainstream outlets only support those who are in the political establishment and who back big corporate interests, not outsiders like Sanders or Trump before he showed his true colors. Ball and Enjeti pride themselves on bringing numerous people from different backgrounds onto their show. They allowed supporters as well as members of both the Sanders and Trump campaigns to have their chance to speak, without being viciously attacked. This provides them with a better understanding of the happenings in our country and furnishes a more complete picture of current events for their audience.

I spoke with Enjeti, and he expanded on why they try to bring as many different people as they can.

"Why would anyone watch *Rising* if it was the same guests as cable news?" Enjeti pondered. "Who cares? It's only interesting if you bring on guests who aren't on cable news, because there are a lot of really interesting people out there who deserve a voice just like everybody else."

The show is broken down into numerous segments: they have a brief introduction where they preview what they will talk about and who will be on the show, followed by a segment titled "On My Radar," a monologue-type bit where they discuss what they think is the most important story at the time and detail their thoughts on the issues. Ball once did one laying out how the mainstream media's corporate bias works, where she discussed how journalists react to group-think, self-interest, and incentives. They then cover a few other stories and follow it up by having a large panel discussion with various different guests.

The segments flow nicely and have the appearance as if they were produced by the mainstream media, but the content is much different. It's more complete and in tune with what is actually happening; this is in large part due to the fact Enjeti and Ball are the ones calling the shots for their show, and they take that responsibility seriously.

"We're totally in charge; we pick all the stories, we write all the headlines, we do everything. Every single topic up there is picked by either me or her," Enjeti said.

He went on to discuss how their thoroughness is a key differentiator between their show and the shows you see on cable news.

"Frankly, we're smarter than them," Enjeti proclaimed. "We are much more nuanced and well-read, and we put a lot more research into our stories. We don't buy pre-baked narratives, so we are always doing research. We don't do anything if we don't know anything about it. That never happens. That's a huge difference between us and cable."

Ball and Enjeti both have experience with the mainstream media, so they are self-aware and know what not to do. Ball was a host on MSNBC's *The Cycle,* and Enjeti was a White

House correspondent for *The Daily Caller*, so they both have been up close and personal with numerous journalists from the mainstream outlets. Ball and Enjeti know the mainstream media lacks objectivity and rarely portrays the whole story. Through bringing numerous guests with different ideas and experiences on *Rising*, they are doing all they can to provide a truly objective and reliable news source for Americans.

"We treat everyone with respect," Enjeti said. "Check it out."

QUICK HITS

Quick Hits News is another alternative to the mainstream media. *Quick Hits* is new to the scene, having been started in early 2020 by a group of journalists including David Shuster, who we all know quite well by now. *Quick Hits* is produced as a daily short ten-to-fifteen-minute clip, where highly experienced journalists discuss the day's top stories. Shuster is the lead anchor, but is accompanied by Tal Heinrich, Arielle Hixson, Antonio Mora, Teresa Krug, Michael Shure, Michael Yam, Rahmah Pauzi, Robert Ray, Randall Pinkston, Joe Williams, Andy Roesgen, Harriet Marsden, Julia Sun, and Sara Hassan. All of these journalists have extensive experience, something Shuster believes sets them apart from other outlets.

Shuster described the beginning of *Quick Hits*, what it is, and what their objective as a news team is.

"Because of COVID-19, everyone is having to broadcast from home," Shuster said. "And we discovered that there was a technology that allowed us to broadcast from home with a pretty good quality too. The difference being instead of being beholden to a large news organization, we could sort of do whatever the hell we wanted at very low production costs.

"What we wanted to do was cover the top ten or twelve stories every day, as opposed to one story hour after hour after hour. Between the journalists I'd worked for at international news stations, who had covered the world and people who had covered a lot of politics, and people who had been at networks for a long time, older people, younger people, black, white, we thought, 'You know what, there's a lane to sort of be what CNN was twenty years ago,' and that is you'd watch for half an hour and you would get all the top stories around the world and across the United States.

"Well you can't do that anymore at CNN or MSNBC or at Fox or at the broadcast networks; they don't cover international news hardly ever," Shuster continued. "So we thought, 'Okay, let's take a group of journalists who all have great experience, are great on air, network-level experience, international experience, and have a passion for both international news and US domestic news and let's do a broadcast each day, fifteen to eighteen minutes now, where we cover top US stories and top international stories and we have someone who knows this stuff.'

"We have an expert who has lived in the Middle East, or we have someone who knows Russia really well, or we have someone who knows Europe really well, or we have one of our correspondents who's actually in London and can talk about what's going on with British Prime Minister Johnson and the lockdown that's taking place. So we have people who are literally in these places, know the story backward and forward, who wouldn't be able to get the kind of airtime in the US, but they're getting a minute and a half, two minutes on our little thing, and they're able to dive into it.

"I don't want to say we're non-biased because if you watch long enough, you'll see that some people come at things with a little more position, some people a little more liberal. There are some disagreements when we get people's reaction to 'is there reason to be optimistic about a vaccine? Should we really believe that Trump is going to have a peaceful transfer of power?' I mean, people have different perspectives in terms of the story they react to, and so you get a little bit of the argument on both sides, but you also get a lot of news."

I interviewed Shuster before Trump left office, so that's why he was talking about the prospects of Trump's transfer of power. As we now know, the answer to the question Shuster proposed is murky at best. Trump may not have been a direct part of it, but the Capital takeover may lead some to think it wasn't a completely nonviolent transfer of power. However, that's not what this is about, so back to Shuster on *Quick Hits*.

"You get a lot of news from the Middle East, from Asia, from Europe from across the United States," Shuster said. "We'll try to get some technology stories in there and we'll always finish each broadcast with a reminder that a lot of people are still inherently good, that there are a lot of good stories that are out there too.

"So we think of it as instead of the broadcast channels and broadcast cable networks and news organizations that will waste your time hour after hour after hour with the same story, or they'll hype things up to such a way that will sort of play with your inner emotions, we're just, 'You know what, here are the ten most interesting stories that we found today, politics, international news, in finance, in science, and here's some of the most interesting pictures we've seen today, and here's the most interesting feel good story.'

"We bring it to people in fifteen to eighteen minutes, in the hopes that people are looking for it in this time where so many of us have had to pare down and simplify our lives because of COVID-19. Having to be at home and social distancing, we think that people just want to know what the news is. They don't want a bunch of people telling them the news is good or the news is bad. They just want a reliable, credible reputation of what are the top stories in the United States and across the world today, by journalists who have experience telling stories and who have an expertise in each of the stories. That's basically *Quick Hits*."

They cover a lot of news in a short amount of time. They don't suck you in with all the bullshit punditry and sensationalism the mainstream media has. *Quick Hits* just gives you the top stories in a very *Quick Hits* fashion.

Another big plus to *Quick Hits* is they are independent. The journalists at *Quick Hits* are currently self-funding their show with money from their own pockets, so they have all the editorial freedom in the world. They are looking for more sustainable long-term funding options and are talking to some organizations about syndicating them, as in paying *Quick Hits* to have their show on the organization's website.

Their idea is if some organizations find it's too expensive to have their own studios and produce their own video news content, they would be willing to syndicate *Quick Hits*. Shuster said they'd been talking to LinkedIn, Facebook, and various news organizations about this. They are also thinking about doing something similar to TYT, where paying subscribers would get bonus coverage and content in addition to the main show, but that has yet to be decided on. The big thing Shuster and his team have decided on is they want to remain independent. They don't want a corporate overlord that threatens their editorial freedom, and with that, the objectivity of their reporting.

"The autonomy is off the charts," Shuster said. "It's the one thing that we are very surely protective of as we move forward with financial arrangements or deals. Our idea is that, okay, if somebody wants a fifteen-minute *Quick Hits* on sports, or fifteen minutes *Quick Hits* on the economy, or on weather, what we're doing is we can replicate our format: conversational, fast reporting using very inexpensive production. Having people at in-home studios, we can do that basically on any topic, and we know enough people in finance, in bitcoin, in currency, that if somebody comes along and says, 'I want a customized sixty-minute every day on finance,' okay, we can do that for you.

"However, we're still very big on, even if you say you want all the stories to be science-related, or stories to be national and international news or just US politics, that it's our editorial control over how we do it and what we do. We're going to be very protective of the autonomy that we have to make sure that we're going to do stories fairly and straight. We're not going to do opinionated fifteen-minute segments. If a fat cat came along and said, 'Here's five million dollars to do a story on how climate change doesn't exist,' we'd tell him, 'You know, go fuck yourself and your five million dollars.' We are going to do things that protect our journalism and our credibility."

Quick Hits is a great alternative to the mainstream media. They have experienced reporters and are independent of corporate interests. Similar to *TYT* and *Rising*, they have experience working in the mainstream media, so they know what people are sick of and what not to do. If you don't have much time but you want to get some real news, check *Quick Hits News* out. You can find them on their website, quickhitstv.com, or YouTube.

TOO MUCH INFORMATION (TMI)/THE DAILY POSTER

Too Much Information is an online newsletter that is published by David Sirota on his website. It has since been expanded into a completely new journalistic venture by name of *The Daily Poster*. At *The Daily Poster*, Sirota, who is the founder and editor-in-chief, and his team perform high-quality, hard-hitting journalism, the kind of journalism that was intended when the Founding Fathers guaranteed the right to a free press.

I spoke to Sirota about his media project before he launched *The Daily Poster*, when it was just his newsletter *TMI*. He described what his motivations behind it were, and those motivations are the same ones that sprouted *The Daily Poster*.

"It started as almost like an experiment, and it has grown exponentially," Sirota said. "Frankly, I'm at a point where I'm a little bit, not confused, but I'm sort of trying to figure out what to do with it and how far I want to take it. We've certainly broken big stories, and I'm really proud of that. Part of it is that I want to do the journalism that I'm doing, and I don't want to answer to corporate masters. I never have, and I don't want to. I'd like it to serve as a testing place and a place to prove that the model of grassroots-funded journalism can work and can be sustainable.

"So far I've been pretty inspired by the response that it's gotten. I honestly didn't expect that it would get the response that it's gotten. I think some of that is clearly whatever notoriety I have from the Bernie campaign. I should mention that I'd done the *Bern Notice* and, like, I've known Bernie for twenty years, and I don't look at politics like 'the election's over, I guess we just fold up shop, the cause is done.' There's a continuity to it that I think if you're serious about building movements, if you run a campaign and you lose, you don't just stop interviewing people, so there's that.

"There's also, can this actually work? Can we get people, grassroots donors, to pitch in, in a way that they see the value of journalism? We've been producing more frequent pieces, somewhat shorter, as opposed to going dark for a while and doing longer pieces. Part of me doesn't love that, because I'd like to do some stuff that's a little more in-depth sometimes, but I also think that the nature of how media is consumed now, you've got to be producing stuff in a short time period."

In the time Sirota had his newsletter *TMI* up and running, he proved it could work, and it was enough to get him to further invest his time by founding *The Daily Poster*. Sirota is able to do hard-hitting journalism the mainstream media shies away from because he's independent from corporate interests. *TMI* and now *The Daily Poster* are 100 percent independent.

Sirota detailed how *TMI* is funded.

"We have subscribers and we have a syndication deal with Jacobin which will run some of our content and kick in as sort of a super-supporter," Sirota told me. "The amount that *Jacobin* ends up giving us is only like 25 or 20 percent of the amount of resources that we've used, so 75 percent is subscribers, 25 percent is *Jacobin*.

"It's 100 percent independent. *Jacobin* is its own publication, so we don't have a rich benefactor, we don't have anything like that, foundation, corporation, we have none of that."

On *The Daily Poster*'s website, they state, "We started this journalism project because we believe in building a new kind of media outlet—one that is independent and 100 percent grassroots-funded, which allows us to do the kind of hard-hitting reporting that corporate-funded media often avoids." [230]

If news in the form of print is your cup of tea, then *The Daily Poster* is a great alternative to the corporate bias that can be found in the big papers like the *New York Times* and *The*

---

230 "About," *The Daily Poster*, accessed January 25, 2021.

Washington Post. Sirota and his team do great journalism. It's why they are despised by so many in the DC establishment. If you want real hard-hitting, objective news in print form, *The Daily Poster* is for you. You can find it at dailyposter.com.

In order to get the high-quality, hard-hitting, wholesome, objective news Americans deserve and require, we must divert from the structure of corporate ownership of the news. We can take a big step in doing this by replacing the corporately owned mainstream media with independent alternatives that are trying to change the structure of our news. *TYT, Rising, Quick Hits*, and *The Daily Poster* are all good, objective, independent sources you can turn to, to get you started in changing your news consuming habits.

CONCLUSION

———

Today in America, we are extremely divided. Republican vs. Democrat, Right vs. Left, the polarization in America is only getting worse, but it shouldn't be. We should be coming together as a nation and demanding a better standard of living for all of us. We fight amongst each other as if our neighbors are the root of our problem, and why wouldn't we think that? It's what we're told in the news, and the news is always the truth, right?

Sadly, that just isn't the case in the United States. The vast majority of Americans are suffering right now. For the first time in our nation's history, we have a generation that is living with a lower standard of living than their parents. People are losing jobs. They're getting sick and dying because of our inadequate healthcare system. Black men are getting gunned down by police and our cities are burning. If someone who didn't know any better walked through America right now, they would think it was a war zone, filled with struggling people just trying to survive. Yet we continue to be the wealthiest nation on the planet.

So why is it we can be the wealthiest country in the world yet still have these massive problems here at home? It's because that wealth isn't going to everyone; it's going to the top of the financial ladder. The fat cats are getting richer while the rest of us suffer. It's been happening for years, but has only been accelerated by the coronavirus pandemic we are living through. As of early August 2020, billionaires in America added 637 billion dollars to their collective fortunes, while forty million Americans filed for unemployment.[231]

How is that allowed to happen in the "greatest country on earth"? It happens because our country is structured to ensure it happens. Not only are the financial elites of this country allowed to purchase political favors by buying politicians through high-dollar campaign contributions, they're also able to divide everyday Americans against themselves. They do this by dictating the public debate in this country by way of the mainstream news media they just so happen to own.

The top dogs of this country own our news media, and this gives them tremendous amounts of power to mold our nation's political discourse in a fashion that is beneficial to them and them alone. The corporately owned mainstream media, through story selection, sensationalism, and blatant censorship, fosters a vicious two-party fight between the right and the left in our country.

---

231 Hiatt Woods, "How Billionaires Saw Their Net Worth Increase by Half a Trillion Dollars during the Pandemic," *Business Insider*, October 30, 2020.

Fox News pushes right-wing Republican perspectives while MSNBC and CNN push Democratic perspectives. However, there is a large caveat to this; all of these networks only favor establishment politicians who are beholden to corporate interests. By doing this, they're able to create a politics where they, the big-monied interests, win every time and the American people lose all the time. They do this by forcing us to choose between a Republican who supports corporate interests over the people and a Democrat who supports corporate interests over the people. Whenever a true champion of the working class rises up, they use the power of the mainstream media to crush them.

As we've explored previously, a prime example of this is Bernie Sanders, a guy who has fought for the working class his entire life. His campaigns for the presidency in both 2016 and 2020 threatened the corporate interests that own our media and control our politicians.

Sanders's politics were for the people. He wanted big corporations to start paying their fair share so everyday Americans could live with the dignity they deserve. The financial elites feared him, so they crushed him by way of their news media, and with that, they crushed any threat to the system they so greatly benefit from.

In the early stages of the 2016 presidential campaign, then presidential candidate Donald Trump was echoing some of the same rhetoric Sanders was, and in response to that, he faced the same opposition from the media Sanders did. The only difference: Trump eventually made it known to his wealthy buddies who own the media he, in fact, was no threat to them, so they eased up on him and he was just another politician in the game. Just one who tweeted a lot and vocalized what had usually been left unsaid.

The root of our problems in this country is not the Trump supporters, the Black Lives Matter protesters, the Sanders supporters, or whatever group you'd like to blame. The root of our problems in this country is the greed of the financial elite who use the mainstream media to take advantage of us: the everyday, hardworking Americans who just want a shot at the American dream.

This increase in polarization, which is by design, leads to one group, largely Republicans, believing everything Fox News says and calling everything that comes from MSNBC and CNN fake news, while the other side does just the opposite. Democrats tend to believe everything reported by MSNBC or CNN, whereas they lament Fox News.

America has always been divided, but this increase in polarization is extremely problematic because the reality of the situation is these networks are much more similar than they are different. This intense tribalism causes people to focus on the deficiencies of the opposing side, all the while turning a blind eye to the many deficiencies in the news outlets they find to be reputable news sources. This dynamic leads to both sides having a distorted view of the truth, and that is not a good thing.

The bottom line is all of the mainstream networks aren't providing their consumers with the whole story. So everyday Americans must stop fighting with one another and calling each other stupid, uneducated, brainwashed, or whatever else it may be. If you get your news from Fox, your enemy isn't the people who watch MSNBC or CNN. If you watch MSNBC or CNN, your enemy isn't the people who watch Fox. It's time to wake up and see we're all being conned.

It is not right-left, it is top-down. Our enemy should not be each other; it should be the financial elites of this country and the system of corporate ownership of the news media that empowers them.

This structure of corporate ownership incentivizes these news organizations not to report the full accurate version of every story; instead, they report in a manner that benefits their owners.

It is important to remember it is not the individual journalists who are at fault for how the mainstream news media acts. The structure of corporate ownership and the structure of corporate ownership alone is to blame.

It influences the news coverage in our country through the use of a system of filtration when hiring journalists and deciding who to promote. If a journalist wants to keep their job and provide for their family, they need to toe the company line and swim in the direction their corporate bosses want them to.

As David Shuster told me, "[Journalists] are made aware of where the channel or the network organization's priorities are. It is made clear to them, don't fuck with the piggy bank, or the people who are buttering your bread."

The phenomenon of groupthink is also at work in mainstream media newsrooms across this country. It acts as a failsafe to make sure that anti-big money sentiment never sees the light of day.

The mainstream media in the United States is not the objective, hard-hitting fourth estate our Founding Fathers intended it to be when they outlined the right to a free press in the Bill of Rights some two hundred thirty years ago in 1791.[232] Rather than working as a check on power like the Founding Fathers intended, our press is instead working to increase the power of the already powerful.

The only way we can change this and get a press that serves the people like the Founding Fathers intended is to come together as a nation and overthrow this structure of corporate ownership of our news media. We can do this by supporting a structure of journalism that incentivizes good, honest, wholesome, objective, and hard-hitting reporting. That structure is grassroots, subscriber-funded journalism.

We need a truly independent press. It won't be easy and it won't happen overnight, but it needs to happen. Fortunately for us, there are independent media outlets that are already fighting this fight and trying to change the economic structure of our news media, but they can't do it alone; they need our help. We can help them by supporting independent outlets, purchasing subscriptions, or making contributions to help them compete with the mainstream media. But most

---

232 "Bill of Rights (1791)," *Our Documents*, accessed January 27, 2021.

importantly, we must trust the independent media outlets more than we trust what we hear in the mainstream media.

The news that comes from the mainstream media is slanted in a way that benefits its owners. It may not be obvious, but that slant is there. We as consumers of the news must identify this so we don't continue to be prey to this corporately controlled system. If we are more critical and aware of this, or just stop watching the mainstream news media altogether, we will be in a much better position to make the right political choices in the future. We will be able to truly pick a candidate to vote for based on what they will do for us, not based on what they will do for corporations. We will be able to examine candidates through our own eyes, not just the corporately controlled eyes of the mainstream media. If we do this, the chances of the politicians we elect actually caring about our livelihoods and standard of living will increase exponentially, and that can only be a good thing.

If you're nervous about the impact such a drastic change could have, I assure you the positive change in our country would more than make up for whatever perceived negatives there could be. By stripping corporations of the power of controlling the media, there would be a much higher chance of a more equitable distribution of wealth in our country, as well as policies that help everyone, not just a few, like Medicare-for-all, college-for-all, and many more. The implementation of these policies in our country would have a much greater and more positive impact on our society than any possible negatives one could think of.

We must call out the corporately owned mainstream media of this country what they are: an instrument the financial elites of this country use to take advantage of us. We must replace them and the structure of corporate ownership with a structure that makes the press beholden to us, the American people. If we are able to do this, and I believe supporting many independent, grassroots-funded journalistic outlets is how we do it, there just might be hope for our country. If we can solve our problem with the news in this country, we can finally educate each other and make our country work for all of us, not just a select few.

ACKNOWLEDGMENTS

Writing a book isn't easy. It takes a lot of time and a lot of effort, but what it requires most of all is people. Writing a book requires the hard work of many people, and my book is no different. That is why it is necessary to acknowledge and thank everyone who helped me during the long journey of writing and publishing this book. Thank you, it means the world to me you all were willing to put in the time, money, and effort to help me shed light on this immense issue facing our country: the current state of the mainstream news media in the United States and how its structure of corporate ownership prevents Americans from receiving the good, honest, objective journalism they deserve.

I would like to specifically thank the individuals who took the time out of their busy lives to answer my many questions for this book. Thank you, David Shuster, Cenk Uygur, David Sirota, and Saagar Enjeti. I appreciate it. My book wouldn't be what it is without you.

I would like to thank everyone at the Creator Institute and New Degree Press, especially Eric Koester, Brian Bies, and my coauthors who helped me in more ways than I can write. Thank you.

I would also like to thank my developmental editor Avery Lockland and my marketing revisions editor John Chancey, who both put in so much time and effort to help make this book what it is today.

In addition to these people, I would like to thank my family and friends who supported me throughout this journey and probably talked about this book a little more than they wanted to. Thank you, I appreciate it more than you know.

Finally, I would like to give a special thanks to the following people:

Hans Arvidson-Hicks	Jonah Gravelle
Dana Bakke	MiChelle Gustafson
Jim Berarducci	Tanner Hagen
Gracie Butchart	Matt & Anne Haugen
Heather Dorsey	Mark Helmer
Luke Dow	Anthony Hendriks
Sandra Evenson	Ray & Stefanie Higgins
Brooke & John Fairbairn	Anna Huffman
Jared Finnerty	Andrew & Maryellen Klemer
John Freeman	Eric Koester
Chris & Shannon Gardner	Rachel Kukielka
Stuart Gardner	Lexi Lanigan
Sean & Kathryn Gavin	Jonathan Laughlin
Iyzaya Gill	David Loobey
Josh Godbout	Michelle & David Lowe
Makaio Goods	Kim Mageau

Sue & Michael Mageau
Tom & Harolyn Mageau
Dave & Paula Jasinski
Ronald Melin
Kenny & Kathy Melin
Krysta Mielke
Jack Norlen
Emily Nothacker
Petra O'Connor
Breanna O'Connor
Kyle O'Connor
Jim & Terry Olson
Amanda Pignato
Rachel Pladson
Cathy Pugh
Susan Quam
Gail Rosenblum

Nathan Sande
Cal Schneider
Brent Sears
Treven Smalley
Emma Spooner
Madison Staggert
Julie & Steve Stelman
Ben Stelman
Christine Stelman-Stefank
Suzanne Sundberg
Jon & Jessica Swaim
Romi Taylor
Rich Updegrove
Jonah Wehr
Madelyn Wuestewald
Paul Zosel

All of these people helped make this book a reality by pre-ordering a copy or contributing to my crowdsourcing campaign. Ultimately, if it wasn't for you, this book wouldn't exist. Thanks to all of you.

Writing and publishing a book is a long and arduous process, and no one can do it alone. From the bottom of my heart, thank you to everyone who helped me along the way.

APPENDIX

INTRODUCTION

Cho, Joshua. "Corporate Media Drove Joe Biden to Victory – but Claims It Doesn't Really Exist." *Salon*, April 25, 2020. https://www.salon.com/2020/04/25/corporate-media-claims-it-I-exist—even-after-driving-joe-biden-to-victory_partner/

James, Meg. "Must Reads: Murdoch Family Launches a New Fox and Former House Speaker Paul Ryan Joins Its Board." *Los Angeles Times*, March 19, 2019. https://www.latimes.com/business/hollywood/la-fi-ct-fox-spinoff-20190319-story.html

Sandler, Rachel, and Gould, Skye. "Here's Everything AT&T Will Own after It Buys TimeWarner" *Business Insider*, June 14, 2018. https://www.businessinsider.com/att-time-warner-acquisition-what-it-will-own-2018-6

Sutton, Kelsey. "Trump Calls CNN 'Fake News,' as Channel Defends Its Reporting on Intelligence Briefing." *Politico*, January 11, 2017. https://www.politico.com/blogs/on-media/2017/01/

trump-refusing-to-answer-question-from-cnn-reporter-you-are-fake-news-233485

U.S. Const. amend. I.

Zacks. "Your Complete Guide to Everything Owned by Comcast." *Nasdaq, Inc.,* October 12, 2017. https://www.nasdaq.com/articles/your-complete-guide-everything-owned-comcast-2017-10-12

CHAPTER 1

Adelman, Joseph M. "Mobilizing the Public against Censorship, 1765 and 2012." *The Atlantic,* January 23, 2012. https://www.theatlantic.com/technology/archive/2012/01/mobilizing-the-public-against-censorship-1765-and-2012/251830/.

Apple Jr., R. W. "25 Years Later; Lessons from the Pentagon Papers." *The New York Times,* June 23, 1996. https://www.nytimes.com/1996/06/23/weekinreview/25-years-later-lessons-from-the-pentagon-papers.html.

Barron, Christina. "No Monument for Madison. But One of His Legacies Is Freedom of the Press." *The Washington Post,* March 14, 2017. https://www.washingtonpost.com/lifestyle/kidspost/no-monument-for-madison-but-one-of-his-legacies-isfreedom-of-the-press/2017/03/14/3847aa5a-01eb-11e7-b9fa-ed727b644a0b_story.html.

Bernstein, Carl, and Bob Woodward. "Bug Suspect Got Campaign Funds." *The Washington Post,* August 1, 1972. https://www.

washingtonpost.com/politics/bug-suspect-got-campaign-funds/2012/06/06/gJQAyTjKJV_story.html.

Bernstein, Carl, and Bob Woodward. "FBI Finds Nixon Aides Sabotaged Democrats." *The Washington Post*, October 10, 1972. https://www.washingtonpost.com/politics/fbi-finds-nixon-aides-sabotaged-democrats/2012/06/06/gJQAoHIJJV_story.html.

Correll, John T. "The Pentagon Papers." *Air Force Magazine*, February 1, 2007. https://www.airforcemag.com/article/0207pentagon/.

CNN. "Cover Story: Pentagon Papers: The Secret War." June 28, 1971. http://edition.cnn.com/ALLPOLITICS/1996/analysis/back.time/9606/28/index.shtml.

United States Department of Defense. "Evolution of the War. Counterinsurgency: The Kennedy Commitments and Programs, 1961." In *The Pentagon Papers.* Volume 2. Pp 1–39. Distributed by *MountHolyoke.* https://www.mtholyoke.edu/acad/intrel/pentagon2/pent1.htm.

History.com Editors. "Pentagon Papers." *History*, August 21, 2018. https://www.history.com/topics/vietnam-war/pentagon-papers.

Oyez. "New York Times Company V. Sullivan." Accessed February 18, 2021. https://www.oyez.org/cases/1963/39.

Oyez. "New York Times Company V. United States." Accessed February 18, 2021. https://www.oyez.org/cases/1970/1873.

The Washington Post. "Part 1 The Post Investigates." In "The Watergate Story." Accessed February 18, 2021. https://www.washingtonpost.com/wp-srv/politics/special/watergate/part1.html.

The US National Archives and Record Administration. "The Bill of Rights: How Did It Happen?" December 14, 2018. https://www.archives.gov/founding-docs/bill-of-rights/how-did-it-happen.

United States Department of Defense. "The Overthrow of NGO Dinh Diem, May-November, 1963." In *The Pentagon Papers.* Volume 2. Pp 201–276. Distributed by *MountHolyoke.* https://www.mtholyoke.edu/acad/intrel/pentagon2/pent6.htm.

Watergate.info. "Watergate: The Scandal That Brought down Richard Nixon." Accessed February 18, 2021. https://watergate.info.

Wermiel, Stephen. "New York Times Co. V. Sullivan (1964)." *The First Amendment Encyclopedia.* Middle Tennessee State University. https://www.mtsu.edu/first-amendment/article/186/new-york-times-co-v-sullivan.

CHAPTER 2

Binelli, Mark. "Keith Olbermann on Why He Left MSNBC – and How He Plans to Get Even." *RollingStone*, June 7, 2011. https://www.rollingstone.com/politics/politics-news/keith-olbermann-on-why-he-left-msnbc-and-how-he-plans-to-get-even-244482/.

Hobson, Jeremy. "How Ted Turner's Vision for CNN Sparked the 24-Hour News Cycle." W*bur*, May 12, 2020. https://www.wbur.org/hereandnow/2020/05/12/cnn-ted-turner-lisa-napoli.

Bravaccio, David, Daniel Shin, Rose Conlon, and Alex Schroeder. "40 Years of CNN, and the Birth of 24-Hour News Coverage." *Marketplace*, June 19, 2020. https://www.marketplace.org/2020/06/19/cnn-40th-birthday-cable-news-business-journalism/.

Carpenter, J. William. "3 Major Companies Owned By Time Warner." *Investopedia*, October 14, 2018. https://www.investopedia.com/articles/markets/102215/top-3-companies-owned-time-warner.asp.

Encyclopedia Britannica, s.v. "CNN," accessed January 19, 2021. https://www.britannica.com/topic/CNN.

MediaVillage. "History's Moment in Media: Aol Time Warner Merger." January 14, 2019. https://www.mediavillage.com/article/historys-moment-in-media-aol-time-warner-merger/.

Institute of Mergers, Acquisitions, and Alliances. "M&A Statistics." Accessed Jan 20, 2021. https://imaa-institute.org/mergers-and-acquisitions-statistics/.

Mulligan, Thomas S. "Turner-Time Warner Merger Approved by Shareholders." *Los Angeles Times*, October 11, 1996. https://www.latimes.com/archives/la-xpm-1996-10-11-fi-52676-story.html.

Pressman, Aaron. "Who Is New AT&T CEO John Stankey?" *Fortune*, April 24, 2020. https://fortune.com/2020/04/24/new-att-ceo-john-stankey-2020/.

Reiff, Nathan. "AT&T and Time Warner Merger Case: What You Need to Know." *Investopedia,* updated December 7, 2018. https://www.investopedia.com/investing/att-and-time-warner-merger-case-what-you-need-know/.

Rifkin, Beth. "The 5 Highest Paid Execs in Telecom." *Investopedia,* March 23, 2020. https://www.investopedia.com/articles/wealth-management/041316/5-highest-paid-executives-telecommunications-sector-s-t.asp.

Romm, Tony, and Brian Fung. "AT&T-Time Warner Merger Approved, Setting the Stage for More Consolidation across Corporate America." *The Washington Post,* June 12, 2018. https://www.washingtonpost.com/news/the-switch/wp/2018/06/12/att-time-warner-decision/.

CHAPTER 3

AdAge. "NBC, Dow Jones Reveal Merger Details." December 10, 1997. https://adage.com/article/news/nbc-dow-jones-reveal-merger-details/12739.

Arango, Tim. "G.E. Makes It Official: NBC Will Go to Comcast." *The New York Times,* December 3, 2009. https://www.nytimes.com/2009/12/04/business/media/04nbc.html.

Blagdon, Jeff. "Microsoft Sells MSNBC.com Stake to Comcast, Will Launch New MSN News Team." *TheVerge,* July 15, 2012. https://www.theverge.com/2012/7/15/3161659/msnbc-acquisition-comcast-redirect-nbcnews.

Carchidi, Sam. "Comcast Buying Remaining Flyers Shares from Snider's Estate." *The Philadelphia Inquirer*, September 22, 2016. https://www.inquirer.com/philly/sports/flyers/20160923_Comcast_buying_remaining_Flyers_shares_from_Snider_s_estate.html.

Carter, Bill. "G.E. Finishes Vivendi Deal, Expanding Its Media Assets." *The New York Times*, October 9, 2003. https://www.nytimes.com/2003/10/09/business/ge-finishes-vivendi-deal-expanding-its-media-assets.html.

Comcast Ventures. "Comcast Ventures." Accessed January 20, 2021. https://comcastventures.com.

Comcast Ventures. "Portfolio." Accessed January 20, 2021. https://comcastventures.com/portfolio.

Friedman, Wayne. "NBC Buys Up More Of MSNBC From Microsoft." *MediaPost,* December 27, 2005. https://www.mediapost.com/publications/article/37854/nbc-buys-up-more-of-msnbc-from-microsoft.html.

Fung, Brian. "Comcast Is Buying Dreamworks in a $3.8 Billion Acquisition." *The Washington Post*, April 28, 2016. https://www.washingtonpost.com/news/the-switch/wp/2016/04/28/comcast-is-buying-dreamworks-in-a-3-8-billion-acquisition/.

James, Meg. "NBC to Acquire Telemundo Network for $1.98 Billion." *Los Angeles Times,* October 12, 2001. https://www.latimes.com/archives/la-xpm-2001-oct-12-fi-56173-story.html.

Jeffries, Adrianne. "The Worst Company in America." *The Verge*, August 19, 2014. https://www.theverge.com/2014/8/19/6004131/comcast-the-worst-company-in-america.

macrotrends. "Comcast Revenue 2006-2020 | CMCSA." Accessed January, 20, 2021. https://www.macrotrends.net/stocks/charts/CMCSA/comcast/revenue?q=NBCUniversal.

Nakashima, Ryan. "Comcast to Buy GE's 49 Pct Stake in NBCuniversal." *MSN Money*, February 12, 2013. Distributed by the Internet Archive Wayback Machine. https://web.archive.org/web/20130216103100/http://money.msn.com/business-news/article.aspx?feed=AP&date=20130212&id=16113978.

NBCUniversal. "Brands." Accessed January 17, 2021. https://www.nbcuniversal.com/brands.

Reuters. "Comcast Corporation CMCSA.O." Accessed January 21, 2021. https://www.reuters.com/companies/CMCSA.O.

Sky. "Sky at a Glance." Accessed January 21, 2021. https://static.skyassets.com/contentstack/assets/bltdc2476c7b6b194dd/blt051348c4db9107b7/5dd3ff72a1b665384d343dea/Sky_Europe's_Leader_in_Entertainment_Insert.pdf.

Variety Staff, "NBC, Microsoft Make News with Joint Venture Cable Web." *Variety,* December 17, 1995. https://variety.com/1995/tv/features/nbc-microsoft-make-news-with-joint-venture-cable-web-99123538/.

Vlessing, Etan. "NBCUniversal Earnings Rise, Management Touts Planned Streaming Service." *The Hollywood Reporter*, January

23, 2019. https://www.hollywoodreporter.com/news/nbcuniversal-earnings-rise-led-by-broadcast-tv-unit-1153299.

Wilkerson, David B., and Steve Goldstein, "Comcast Scores Controlling Stake in NBC Universal." *MarketWatch*, December 3, 2009. https://www.marketwatch.com/story/comcast-to-buy-nbc-stake-as-venture-formed-2009-12-03.

Young, Steve. "MSNBC Launches Network." *CNNMoney*, July 15, 1996. https://money.cnn.com/1996/07/15/bizbuzz/msnbc_pkg/.

CHAPTER 4

AP. "News Corp Formally Splits in Two." *USA Today*, updated June 28, 2013. https://www.usatoday.com/story/money/business/2013/06/28/news-corp-to-split-after-Friday-close/2473827/.

Biography. "Rupert Murdoch Biography." Updated June 29, 2020. https://www.biography.com/business-figure/rupert-murdoch.

BBC. "News Corp Officially Splits in Two." June 28, 2013. https://www.bbc.com/news/business-23104822.

Broadcasting. "Another Spin for TV's Revolving Door." May 6, 1985. 39–40. Via World Radio History. https://worldradiohistory.com/Archive-BC/BC-1985/BC-1985-05-06.pdf.

Curtis, Bryan. "The Great NFL Heist: How Fox Paid for and Changed Football Forever." *The Ringer*, December 13, 2018. https://www.theringer.com/nfl/2018/12/13/18137938/nfl-fox-deal-rupert-murdoch-1993-john-madden-terry-bradshaw-howie-long-jimmy-johnson-cbs-nbc.

Dickinson, Tim. "How Roger Ailes Built the Fox News Fear Factory." *RollingStone*, May 25, 2011. https://www.rollingstone.com/politics/politics-news/how-roger-ailes-built-the-fox-news-fear-factory-244652/.

Fallows, James. "The Age of Murdoch." *The Atlantic*, September 2003. https://www.theatlantic.com/magazine/archive/2003/09/the-age-of-murdoch/302777/.

Financial Times. "Interview Transcript: Rupert Murdoch and Roger Ailes." October 6, 2006. https://www.ft.com/content/5b77af92-548c-11db-901f-0000779e2340.

Gray, Tim, and Pat Saperstein, "Fox Merges with Disney: The Storied Studio's 102-Year History." *Variety*, December 14, 2017. https://variety.com/2017/film/news/fox-disney-merger-history-timeline-1202636152/.

Joyella, Mark. "Fox News Marks 17 Years at No. 1, but MSNBC's Rachel Maddow Beats Sean Hannity." *Forbes*, January 29, 1998. https://www.forbes.com/sites/markjoyella/2019/01/29/fox-news-marks-17-years-at-1-but-msnbcs-rachel-maddow-beats-sean-hannity/?sh=65ee37026733.

McNamee, Gregory Lewis. "The Simpsons." *Encyclopedia Britannica*, updated August 13, 2020. https://www.britannica.com/topic/The-Simpsons.

Nelson, John. "Rupert Murdoch Earned His Fox Television Network Instant Respe." *The Associated Press*, December 19, 1993. https://apnews.com/article/4f086b8a49d5978fe5bb3fc8e9e-b8ae9.

Schrage, Michael. "Murdoch Agrees to Buy a 50 Percent Share of
20th Century Fox Film." *The Washington Post,* March 21, 1985.
https://www.washingtonpost.com/archive/business/1985/03/21/
murdoch-agrees-to-buy-a-50-percent-share-of-20th-century-
fox-film/8862819b-50de-4ad3-aeb5-70ca84f109f1/.

21st Century Fox Careers. "Our Brands: FX Networks And Productions." Accessed January 20, 2021. https://foxcareers-staging.
azurewebsites.net/OurBrands/FXNetworksandProductions.

The Associated Press. "New Fox Network Signs up 79 TV Stations
across U.S." *The New York Times,* August 4, 1986. https://www.
nytimes.com/1986/08/04/arts/new-fox-network-signs-up-79-
tv-stations-across-us.html.

The Walt Disney Company. "The Walt Disney Company to Acquire
Twenty-First Century Fox, Inc., after Spinoff of Certain Businesses, for $52.4 Billion in Stock." December 14, 2017. https://
thewaltdisneycompany.com/walt-disney-company-acquire-
twenty-first-century-fox-inc-spinoff-certain-businesses-52-4-
billion-stock-2/.

CHAPTER 5

Berr, Jonathan. "Here Is Everything You Need to Know about the
Viacom-CBS Merger." *Forbes,* November 26, 2019. https://www.
forbes.com/sites/jonathanberr/2019/11/26/here-is-everything-
you-need-to-know-about-the-viacom-cbs-merger/amp/.

Brennan, Jude. "CBS Films' Presidency: And Then There Was One."
Forbes, July 23, 2014. https://www.forbes.com/sites/judebren-

nan/2014/07/23/cbs-films-presidency-and-then-there-was-one/amp/.

Bezos Expeditions. "Bezos Expeditions." Accessed January 21, 2021. https://www.bezosexpeditions.com.

CBS/AP. "CBS, Viacom Formally Split." *CBSNEWS*, January 3, 2006. https://www.cbsnews.com/news/cbs-viacom-formally-split/.

Clifford, Catherine. "Tech Billionaires from Bezos to Benioff Are Buying Media Companies, but 'New York Times Is Not for Sale.'" *CNBC Make It,* updated November 8, 2018. https://www.cnbc.com/2018/11/07/billionaires-are-buying-media-companies-new-york-times-not-for-sale.html.

Farhi, Paul. "Washington Post to Be Sold to Jeff Bezos, the Founder of Amazon." *The Washington Post,* August 5, 2013. https://www.washingtonpost.com/national/washington-post-to-be-sold-to-jeff-bezos/2013/08/05/ca537c9e-fe0c-11e2-9711-3708310f6f4d_story.html.

Forbes. "#1 Jeff Bezos." January 21, 2021. https://www.forbes.com/profile/jeff-bezos/.

Forbes. "#804 Sumner Redstone." Accessed January 20, 2021. https://www.forbes.com/profile/sumner-redstone/.

Funding Universe. "National Amusements Inc. History." Accessed January 20, 2021. http://www.fundinguniverse.com/company-histories/national-amusements-inc-history/.

Funding Universe. "The New York Times Company History." Accessed January 20, 2021. http://www.fundinguniverse.com/company-histories/the-new-york-times-company-history/.

Funding Universe. "Viacom Inc. History." Accessed January 20, 2021. http://www.fundinguniverse.com/company-histories/viacom-inc-history/.

Goldman, M. Corey, and Tom Johnson. "Viacom Tunes in to CBS." *CNNMoney,* September 7, 1999. https://money.cnn.com/1999/09/07/deals/cbs/.

Good Morning America. "Countdown to 'Star Wars: The Rise of Skywalker.'" *ABCNEWS,* December 15, 2019. Video, 3:36. https://abcnews.go.com/GMA/Culture/video/countdown-star-wars-rise-skywalker-67740855.

Hallman, Carly. "Every Company Disney Owns: A Map of Disney's Worldwide Assets." *TitleMax,* accessed January 21, 2021. https://www.titlemax.com/discovery-center/money-finance/companies-disney-owns-worldwide/.

Haselton, Todd. "Disney Bans Netflix Ads from All of Its TV Channels except ESPN." *CNBC,* October 4, 2019. https://www.cnbc.com/2019/10/04/disney-to-ban-netflix-ads-from-all-of-its-tv-services-except-espn-wsj.html.

Henney, Megan. "A Look at Jeff Bezos' Biggest Assets." *FOXBusiness,* April 4, 2019. https://www.foxbusiness.com/business-leaders/a-look-at-jeff-bezos-biggest-assets.

Hofmeister, Sallie, and Jane Hall. "CBS Agrees to Buyout Bid by Westinghouse: Entertainment: $5.4-Billion Merger Would Create Biggest TV, Radio Empire. But the Deal Faces Obstacles." *Los Angeles Times*, August 2, 1995. https://www.latimes.com/archives/la-xpm-1995-08-02-mn-30646-story.html.

inspiringquotes.us. "'The Buck Stops with the Guy Who Signs the Checks.'" Accessed January 21, 2021. https://www.inspiringquotes.us/quotes/Uml6_lYvRuWfg.

Moskowitz, Dan. "The 10 Richest People in the World." *Investopedia*, updated January 25, 2021. https://www.investopedia.com/articles/investing/012715/5-richest-people-world.asp.

NewsCorp. "About Us." Accessed January 21, 2021. https://newscorp.com/about/.

New World Encyclopedia. s.v. "American Broadcasting Company." Accessed January 21, 2021. https://www.newworldencyclopedia.org/entry/American_Broadcasting_Company.

NoCable. "History Timeline of ABC." Accessed January 21, 2021. https://nocable.org/timeline/abc-history.

Parenti, Michael. "Inventing Reality." Accessed January 21, 2021. https://www.youtube.com/watch?v=CHwr2Y7mbhc.

Roberts, Chalmers M. "Eugene Meyer Bought Post 50 Years Ago." *The Washington Post*, June 1, 1983. https://www.washingtonpost.com/archive/politics/1983/06/01/eugene-meyer-bought-post-50-years-ago/910a718e-e71f-46bd-9ad7-78ad9e2107b2/.

Schneider, John F. "Remembering CBS Radio's Beginnings." *RADIOWORLD*, updated July 15, 2020. https://www.radioworld.com/news-and-business/remembering-cbs-radios-beginnings.

Sherman, Alex. "Sumner Redstone Handed a Media Empire to His Daughter, Shari, Who Now Controls Its Fate." *CNBC*, updated August 12, 2020. https://www.cnbc.com/2020/08/12/shari-redstone-now-fully-controls-the-fate-of-viacomcbs.html.

ViacomCBS. "Making Connections around the World." Accessed January 21, 2021. https://www.viacomcbs.com/brands.

ViacomCBS Press Express. "CBS At 75 Feature: CBS Timeline of Milestones." October 23, 2003. https://www.viacomcbspress-express.com/cbs-entertainment/releases/view?id=5134.

wallmine. "Arthur Sulzberger Net Worth." Updated January 1, 2021. https://wallmine.com/nyse/nyt/officer/2105038/arthur-sulzberger.

PART 3

Denchak, Melissa. "Flint Water Crisis: Everything You Need to Know." *NRDC*, November 8, 2018. https://www.nrdc.org/stories/flint-water-crisis-everything-you-need-know.

Wu, Nicholas. "'John Yang?' Andrew Yang Pokes Fun at MSNBC for Flubbing His Name in Broadcast." *USA Today*, September 10, 2019. https://www.usatoday.com/story/news/politics/2019/09/10/john-yang-andrew-yang-jokes-nbc-and-msnbc-name-mix-up/2272208001/.

CHAPTER 6 PART 1

Bret Baier. "Bret Baier." Accessed January 25, 2021. https://www. bretbaier.com.

Shuster, David. "David Shuster." Linkedin, Accessed January 25, 2021. https://www.linkedin.com/in/david-shuster-3a25862/.

CHAPTER 6 PART 2

Ford, Rebecca. "Cenk Uygur Tells Keith Olbermann That MSNBC Trades Truth for Access (Video)." *The Hollywood Reporter,* July 22, 2011. https://www.hollywoodreporter.com/news/cenk-uygur-tells-keith-olbermann-214424.

Madlena, Chavala. "Cenk Uygur on the Success of the Young Turks." *The Guardian,* April 26, 2010. https://www.theguardian.com/media/2010/apr/26/cenk-uygur-young-turks.

Rutz, David. "Ed Schultz Suggests MSNBC Fired Him Because of Bernie Sanders Support." April 16, 2018. Video, 8:59. https://youtu.be/x5ciT778x78.

Sandomir, Richard. "Ed Schultz, Blunt-Spoken Political Talk-Show Host, Dies at 64." *The New York Times,* July 5, 2018. https://www.nytimes.com/2018/07/05/obituaries/ed-schultz-blunt-spoken-political-talk-show-host-dies-at-64.html.

Sheffield, Matthew. "Krystal Ball: MSNBC Never Wanted Ed Schultz's Working Class Audience." *The Hill.* July 6, 2018. https://thehill.com/hilltv/rising/395792-krystal-ball-msnbc-never-wanted-ed-schultzs-working-class-audience.

CHAPTER 7

Cherry, Kendra. "What Is Groupthink?" *verywellmind*, updated November 12, 2020. https://www.verywellmind.com/what-is-groupthink-2795213.

Greenwald, Glenn (@ggreenwald). "Many journalists - either for self-serving reasons or due to genuine befuddlement - are completely misinterpreting Bernie's media critique." Twitter video, August 13, 2019. https://twitter.com/ggreenwald/status/1161425971448373249.

Shafer, Jack, and Tucker Doherty. "The Media Bubble Is Worse Than You Think." *PoliticoMagazine*, May/June 2017. https://www.politico.com/magazine/story/2017/04/25/media-bubble-real-journalism-jobs-east-coast-215048.

Schulte, Gabriela. "Poll: 69 Percent of Voters Support Medicare for All." *The Hill*. April 24, 2020. https://thehill.com/hilltv/what-americas-thinking/494602-poll-69-percent-of-voters-support-medicare-for-all.

CHAPTER 8

Adamczyk, Alicia. "More Billionaires Are Donating to Hillary Clinton Than Donald Trump." *Money,* September 26, 2016. https://money.com/election-2016-billionaires-hillary-clinton/.

Budryk, Zack. "Sanders, Klobuchar among Five Most Popular Senators: Poll." *The Hill,* April 25, 2019. https://thehill.com/homenews/senate/440665-sanders-klobuchar-among-five-most-popular-senators-poll.

Bowden, John. "Poll: Sanders Most Popular Senator, Flake Least." *The Hill*, January 10, 2019. https://thehill.com/homenews/senate/424806-poll-sanders-most-popular-senator-flake-least.

Celebrity Net Worth. "Chris Matthews Net Worth." Accessed January 25, 2021. https://www.celebritynetworth.com/richest-celebrities/chris-matthews-net-worth/.

Ecarma, Caleb. "Joe Biden, Revenant, Was an Irresistible Media Story—and It Helped Win Him Super Tuesday." *Vanity Fair*, March 5, 2020. https://www.vanityfair.com/news/2020/03/joe-biden-media-story-helped-win-him-super-tuesday.

Greenwald, Glenn. "MSNBC Yet Again Broadcasts Blatant Lies, This Time about Bernie Sanders's Opening Speech, and Refuses to Correct Them." *The Intercept*, March 3, 2019. https://theintercept.com/2019/03/03/msnbc-yet-again-broadcasts-blatant-lies-this-time-about-bernie-sanders-opening-speech-and-refuses-to-correct-them/.

Halper, Katie. "MSNBC's Anti-sanders Bias Makes It Forget How to Do Math." *Fair*, July 26, 2019. https://fair.org/home/msnbcs-anti-sanders-bias-makes-it-forget-how-to-do-math/.

Higdon, Nolan, and Mickey Huff. "The Bernie Blackout Is Real, and These Screenshots Prove It." *Truthout,* January 30, 2020. https://truthout.org/articles/the-bernie-blackout-is-real-and-these-screenshots-prove-it/.

Hollar, Julie. "Here's the Evidence Corporate Media Say Is Missing of Wapo Bias against Sanders." *Fair*, August 15, 2019. https://

fair.org/home/heres-the-evidence-corporate-media-say-is-missing-of-wapo-bias-against-sanders/.

Johnstone, Caitlin. "Former MSNBC Reporter Spills Details on Pro-establishment Bias in Media." *Caitlin Johnstone*, August 15, 2019. https://caityjohnstone.medium.com/former-msn-bc-reporter-spills-details-on-pro-establishment-bias-in-media-c1524e6fde2f.

Norton, Dan. "Comcast Exec to Hold Fundraiser for Hillary Clinton." *Philadelphia Business Journal*, updated June 12, 2015. https://www.bizjournals.com/philadelphia/news/2015/06/12/comcast-exec-david-cohen-clinton-fundraiser.html.

David Ruts. "Ed Schultz Suggests MSNBC Fired Him Because of Bernie Sanders Support." April 16, 2018. Video, 8:59. https://www.youtube.com/watch?v=x5ciT778x78&feature=youtu.be.

Savage, Luke. "The Corporate Media's War against Bernie Sanders Is Very Real." *Jacobin*, November 20, 2019. https://www.jacobinmag.com/2019/11/corporate-media-bernie-sanders-bias-msnbc-warren-biden.

Schwartz, Ian. "Chuck Todd Cites Quote Calling Sanders Supporters 'Digital Brownshirt Brigade.'" *RealClear Politics*, February 10, 2020. https://www.realclearpolitics.com/video/2020/02/10/chuck_todd_cites_quote_calling_sanders_supporters_digital_brownshirt_brigade.html.

The Texas Politics Project. "Free Media versus Earned Media." *University of Texas at Austin*, accessed January 26, 2021. https://

texaspolitics.utexas.edu/archive/html/vce/features/0903_01/
freemedia.html.

Wade, Peter. "Chris Matthews' Wild Rant Connects a Bernie
Sanders Win with Public Executions." *RollingStone*, February
8, 2020. https://www.rollingstone.com/politics/politics-news/
chris-matthews-bernie-sanders-public-executions-949802/.

Wu, Nicholas. "'John Yang?' Andrew Yang Pokes Fun at MSNBC
for Flubbing His Name in Broadcast." *USA Today*, September 10, 2019. https://www.usatoday.com/story/news/
politics/2019/09/10/john-yang-andrew-yang-jokes-nbc-and-
msnbc-name-mix-up/2272208001/.

CHAPTER 9

Ariens, Chris. "Here Are the Biggest Advertisers on Fox News,
CNN and MSNBC." *TVNewser*, March 9, 2018. https://www.
adweek.com/tvnewser/here-are-the-biggest-advertisers-on-
fox-news-cnn-and-msnbc/359057/.

CHAPTER 10 PART 1

TedX Talks. "Who Owns the News?" June 26, 2018. Video, 17:22.
https://www.youtube.com/watch?v=b9yAUiJZjLQ.

CHAPTER 10 PART 2

Blattberg, Eric. "The Young Turks Is Running Circles around News
Networks on YouTube." *DigDay*, October 31, 2014. https://digi-
day.com/media/the-young-turks-interview/.

Madlena, Chavala. "Cenk Uygur on the Success of the Young Turks." *The Guardian,* April 26, 2010. https://www.theguardian.com/media/2010/apr/26/cenk-uygur-young-turks.

The Daily Poster. "About." Accessed January 25, 2021. https://www.dailyposter.com/about?utm_source=subscribe_email&utm_content=learn_more.

TOPIO Networks. "TYT Network." Accessed January 25, 2020. https://www.topionetworks.com/companies/tyt-network-598b0b071dedae41c68cd967.

Wulfsohn, Joseph. "New York Times Issues Correction after Suggesting Cenk Uygur Defended David Duke." *Fox News,* December 17, 2019. https://www.foxnews.com/media/ny-times-issues-correction-after-wrongfully-suggesting-cenk-uygur-defended-david-duke.

CONCLUSION

Our Documents. "Bill of Rights (1791)." Accessed January 27, 2021. https://www.ourdocuments.gov/doc.php?flash=true&doc=13.

Woods, Hiatt. "How Billionaires Saw Their Net Worth Increase by Half a Trillion Dollars during the Pandemic." *Business Insider,* October 30, 2020. https://www.businessinsider.com/billionaires-net-worth-increases-coronavirus-pandemic-2020-7.